IDEAL BIRTH

Sondra Ray

Second Edition

Celestial Arts
Berkeley, California

A NOTE OF CAUTION

This book represents advanced and enlightened ideas about the traditions surrounding human birth. These ideas are presented for your consideration and should be discussed with your obstetrician and all other birthing professionals who will attend your delivery. *This material is meant to enhance the birth experience and is in no way intended as a substitute for medical care.*

Second Edition, 1986.

Cover Art by Catherine Andrews
    3111 Third Ave., Santa Monica, CA 90405
Cover Design by Ken Scott
Book Design by Betsy Bruneau Jones
Typography by HMS Typography, Inc.

Manufactured in the United States of America

Library of Congress Cataloging-in-Publication Data

Ray, Sondra.
    Ideal birth.

    Bibliography: p.
    1. Natural childbirth.   I. Title.
[DNLM: 1. Labor—popular works.   2. Natural Childbirth.
3. Pregnancy—popular works.   WQ 150 R264i]
RG661.R38 1985   618.2   84-71025
ISBN: 0-89087-364-X

2 3 4 5 6 — 90 89 88 87 86

Dedication

I dedicate this book to my goddaughter Mela Noel, who waited until she could be born underwater, in Austin, Texas on November 5, 1980. May she be an inspiration to other beings who want to come here in this way. I also acknowledge her parents, Rima and Steve, who were brave enough and alert enough to give her what she wanted and who were pioneers for this important work on the planet.

I dedicate this book to all future souls who wish to be born to conscious parents who are willing to provide for them the holiest atmosphere possible.

In gratitude

Major parts of this book were written in the presence of my guru Babaji, in the Himalaya foothills.

Special thanks to Barbara Keller, Dr. Thomas Verny and Dr. Michel Odent for their contributions to this book.

Prayer For This Book

May everything I write be something beautiful for God! May people read this book and be conscious of improving the birth process in this world, even if they do not plan to be pregnant. May people realize that improving birth practices will improve the world we all live in and the one our children will be living in. May everyone take responsibility for making a contribution of some sort just because he or she is a citizen concerned about the world, about making a difference, and about pursuing excellence.

May it be possible that young women somehow become conscious about being more enlightened in future deliveries of their children, and thus affect the future generations. I pray that this information be shared in high schools, in family sociology courses, or in whatever way is appropriate. (Why should high school girls learn only about menstruation and not about proper ways to prepare for the birth of their future children?) I need help in locating the people who could do this, if it is to be done.

May we provide, for those future beings who are waiting to come here, the safest, sanest and most humane births, giving them the best possible introduction to the world. May we as Rebirthers be a major part of making this safety happen; and if this is to be, let us never be at war with the medical profession. Let us work together in an inspiring way that has never been done, for the good of all. May I bring forth the inspiration for this to occur somehow so that everyone wins. The world wins. May those of us involved in this work have the right motivation.

May all the people who can make this happen begin to come together now. May the Congress of Pre- and Peri-Natal Psychology be always blessed at least as much as it was this year. May everyone in this work be blessed. May every mother delivering a baby be blessed and every baby coming here to us be blessed, even just a little more than before.

Letter to my Readers

Dear Friends,

This book is for anyone who was ever born. Although it may have the most value for people planning a family, it will help anyone to stimulate and clear birth memories. My prayer is that it will also inspire all of you to get rebirthed and to read the other books we have in the Rebirthing community.

After years of trying to erase birth trauma, I felt it was my duty to write a book that would help prevent it in future generations. I used the title *Ideal Birth* because I like to think in terms of Utopia. Being a Futurist, I entertain all possibilities. Also, it is part of my spiritual mission to be a catalyst, inspiring people to go for the best and the highest spiritual thoughts that will contribute to quality of life. I do not mean to imply that underwater birth is the only birth that can be Ideal, however. The most important thing for creating any Ideal situation regarding birth is clarity of consciousness. The important thing is to "tune into" and listen to the baby's request as to what type of birth it wants!

I had the great honor to be able to write most of this book in the presence of my guru, the beloved Shri Shri 1008 Shri Bhagwan Herakhan Wale Baba or Babaji, the hero of the book *Autobiography of a Yogi* (Los Angeles: Self Realization Fellowship, 1971). When you read what it was like for me to write this book I think you will be amazed at the significance of this. I also find it amazing how many times this manuscript dematerialized and rematerialized. It seemed to have a mind of its own and would not allow itself to be completed until a certain significant date, June 1984, the very time Babaji himself told me that world purification, and thus the new world, would begin. Also, the proofs would not catch up to me on the world tour until New Zealand, where so much underwater birth had taken place, where the dolphins had participated in underwater births, and where the ancient Maoris had done birth rituals in water!

Love,
Sondra Ray

P.S. Please pass this book on to anyone planning a family and to anyone interested in clearing their own birth trauma.

Thank you.

Why Should You Read This Book If You Are Neither Pregnant Nor Planning To Be Pregnant?

Do you care about the world? Of course you do. I don't want to *convince* you that caring about birth practices will affect the quality of your life, whether you have a baby or not. I would rather *inspire* you to realize this.

Aren't you quite willing to have better food, better-made clothes and furniture, better entertainment, better art, better landscaping, better-quality relationships, better health? I am sure that you are. Very simply, the better any being on the planet is, the better the quality of your life is. We must all inspire each other to do better so we can serve each other better. One of the ways to create better beings is to give them better births. We must all be responsible for this as a nation! Are we a nation of peace? Then we must have each individual at peace. But how can we be at peace when birth remains a BATTLE, an EMERGENCY, a PAINFUL SITUATION? I like to meditate upon how changing birth practices will improve the world. After years and years of Rebirthing, it is easy for me to see this connection and I hope you will think about it too.

One nation strong in the ways of peace leads the world by showing the way. One city flourishing in peace sets an example to the nation.

One man of peace can save a city.

Is it you?

(Masters of Destiny)

To the Obstetrics Profession

This book offers a supplement to the body of knowledge acquired over the past 100 years in the practice of assisting childbirth. It is intended to restore human sensitivity to the lifesaving technology of modern medicine.

The information assembled here supports an optimum natural birth and gives a model or context within which the tools of the obstetrician and perinatal nurse or midwife can be employed with tact and an eye for necessity.

Please read this book with an open heart and mind. It is in the hospitals and within the medical profession that the quickest changes can be made for the benefit of the greatest numbers of people. Examine the testimonies of your fellow professionals in the book and note the observations and realizations that led them to modify their professional priorities.

Birth is the first and greatest change in life, and because of our subconscious fear of birth we may, by association, fear change itself. As custodians of change, natal physicians and midwives must learn to welcome and cultivate responsible change in their own lives. We do not need to control life, but rather to trust it more, that it may continue to teach us how we may best support its marvelous designs.

Fredric Lehrman
February, 1984

Contents

PART II

PART III

PART IV

PART V

APPENDIX I

APPENDIX II

Preface

The main purpose of this book is to reduce or prevent prenatal trauma and birth trauma to the newborn, and to make the delivery as easy and as "conscious" as possible for everyone concerned.

After six years of rebirthing, a spiritual purification process that is instrumental in clearing up birth trauma, I realized prevention would be an even greater mission for me to endeavor. I tried to imagine the most perfect birth—the most ideal, Utopian and spiritual pregnancy and birth. This book does not intend to say that the only ideal birth is underwater birth (the Russian method). At this time it is impractical for most people to create an underwater birth, so that subject is only one portion of the book. However, it is important to know about and consider it. As a "futurist," I feel we must consider the latest research on any subject. I acknowledge the rebirthing community for its bravery in experimenting with underwater birth, and for its success!

I thank the professionals and obstetricians who have contributed to this book in an attempt to help make hospital births more conscious and enlightened. I ask you to please spread the word and get this book to those planning a baby and to anyone in the field of obstetrics and delivery. This is how you can directly affect the future of the world. Thank you.

Sondra Ray

Foreword

Several years ago Sondra Ray and I were brought together by Divine guidance to help one another on our spiritual paths. My research into physical purification as a means of bringing body into balance and harmony synchronized with her research into etheric purification through loving relationships. Sondra's knowledge and experience in using the science of the breath and her loving efforts in working me through my own birth experiences helped me to move quickly through many levels of clarification; she may have saved me years of work. Further, her persistence in encouraging my participation in the development of the underwater birthing process in the United States led me into areas I never could have comprehended without that purification.

Our first participation in underwater birth was with a mother we met only a few weeks before her due date. In spite of an exceptionally long labor, the experience resulted in a beautiful birth; however, the placenta was retained. After approximately ninety minutes, it became evident that the placenta was not going to deliver without assistance, and the mother was taken by paramedics to a nearby hospital. (The baby stayed at home with the father.) Subsequent interviews with the mother about her experience and previous history led to the discovery that she gave birth to her first child in a very unusual way. She suddenly went into very painful labor at home, alone, and could not get to the telephone. After the baby delivered, she reached the phone with the baby, cord and placenta still attached and called her mother for assistance. Her mother became hysterical, called the paramedics, and met them at the hospital. Her continued criticism about her daughter's stupidity in giving birth at home set up the matrix in her unconscious that one must be in the hospital to complete a birth. During her underwater birth, she was pro grammed to create a situation to go to the hospital *to make her mother happy.*

This led us to decide that we must work with a pregnant woman a minimum of three months to prepare her for an underwater or a natural childbirth, if it were to be an ideal birth experience. Each succeeding birth and subsequent debriefing of the mother confirmed that we should begin working with the mother *as early as possible* to bring to the surface and eliminate from her unconscious all elements that might prevent the perfect birth.

Ultimately, we realized that the time to begin preparation was one year prior to the conception of the child!

Women must now recognize the awesome privilege and responsibility that God has entrusted to them in the co- creation of humanity for the positive evolution of our species. Because their thoughts, feelings, and actions are literally imprinted upon the developing fetus within their wombs, they are "in the image and likeness of God," in that they are actually *creating* the substance and potential of their future child. Many women in the past have allowed this Divine process to occur unconsciously. Now, with the aid of books such as this one, women have the knowledge and the understanding to undertake this joyful task consciously.

This is why it is so imperative for a woman to work on herself, with dedicated purpose and persistence, prior to the conception of her baby. This will give her enough time to let any unconscious elements in her psyche rise to her adult, conscious mind, so that she can rid herself of any personal laws she recognizes as unproductive, both for her own and her future child's well-being. She must learn the self-discipline required to master the control of her thoughts and feelings, thus allowing only what is beautiful, good and true to occupy her consciousness. This takes practice and determination, and should be mastered before pregnancy for optimum results, which will be manifested in children of great intelligence, high moral fiber, and spiritual devotion and integrity, who will delight in serving God through humanity and its new one-world awareness.

The dynamic advances of science in recent decades, together with the rapid development of human potential, are creating revolutionary changes that promise to transform the nature of civilization and form a new society. This underscores the urgency of investigating the implications of these discoveries on the social and human roots of civilization.

Lord Bacon, when referring to the tendency of the old civilization to resist change, called it "the power of the familiar." Comfort for the average person has been to keep operating with thought patterns that have developed over a lifetime. This average person's life is really a series of mistakes that, though there has been opportunity to correct them, have gone uncorrected. In Hollywood a movie company may film a sequence and, when it is not acceptable, call it a mis-take and immediately do a re-take. However, most people simply build up guilt about their mis-takes and never schedule any re-takes. With that guilt, they develop an attitude about themselves that becomes their personality. The effort to maintain this status quo, to remain comfortable with these old patterns of thinking based upon guilt-ridden mis-takes, is what has prevented humanity from developing its fullest potential.

People are trying to live today with forty- to sixty-year-old patterns of thinking, established prior to adulthood, and most are unwilling to change them. We search for the familiar without recognizing that in 1945 we ended a way of life that seemed to offer "security." We used to plan for the future, building homes and families as part of the social structure. In 1945 we became a part of a way of thinking that is not only dangerous but also unethical when we eliminated Hiroshima from planet Earth with nuclear fission. The family unit began disappearing, and life has come to represent instant gratification without regard for the after-effects. We have developed a pattern that produces no security when we look inside, and only thoughts of total destruction on the outside. With that pattern as the basis of our personality, we attempt to get whatever we can to gratify ourselves now—without regard to the metaphysical disturbances we are creating for our children.

We are trying to force the past upon the future, instead of

using the mistakes of the past to build a new foundation for the future. We cannot construct a building without a solid foundation, and we must understand this principle to establish a new foundation for a secure life on this planet. We must reverse the trend of birthing children into trauma and fear before we can create a society with secure thoughts.

We are moving forward with psychic research projects and the development of human potential; but now we must also focus our attention on *how to begin life totally conscious.*

The use of mental imaging—deliberately exploiting the child's ability to receive information *in utero*—is proving to be a phenomenon unique to our times. Some ancient cultures encouraged the pregnant woman to refrain from observing ugly situations or experiencing shock, even to the point of insisting on herbally induced abortion should such events occur. They acted with an instinctual knowledge of how to prevent mentally retarded or deformed humans; however, the positive use of this knowledge in the area of biosophical eugenics is still obscure.

Dr. Igor Tjarkovsky of the USSR pioneered research efforts in the study of the effects of prenatal communication between mother and fetus and between dolphins and fetus. This work usually manifests as an ideal birth in water. The children born from such births have an all-new philosophy about life and live without fear or angry thoughts, even if they were to be physically attacked. If one of these children has a toy that is admired by another child, I have seen that it gives them great pleasure to simply give the toy to their playmate. We are now documenting the work that has been quietly progressing in the Soviet Union for twenty-five years.

Increasing numbers of couples around the world, many of whom we have had the privilege of working with, are now dedicating themselves to preconception preparation—physically, mentally, and spiritually—and the education of the child from the moment of conception through the prenatal period. Some further choose to participate in conscious water birthing. It is a good sign for the future of our planet.

The experiences you are about to witness are the first accounts of children being born as a result of their parents' participating in this new ideology. What you will read in this book is not a fad or simply an attempt to start a new birthing technique, but is rather a whole new philosophy about creating conscious life on this planet. The inter-relationship between physical and psychological motherhood is vitally necessary to the understanding of the enlightened human, who has the conscious knowledge of the collective human experience. It is through such immortalized vehicles that we will create a microcosmic "collective consciousness" to facilitate the planet Earth's rebirth experience.

Daniel Fritz, Managing Director
Jia Lighthouse
Hawaii Prenatal
P.O. Box 727
Molokai, Hawaii 96748
(808) 558-8982

Introduction

Having rebirthed thousands of people over the last six years, and researched the effects of their Birth Trauma on their lives and bodies, I feel more grateful than ever to have this tool and be able to share it with others. I feel proud of my true life's work; and yet I think the greatest contribution would be to prevent the birth trauma in the first place, rather than trying to heal it later. Eight years earlier I came to the same conclusion when I gave up fourteen years of nursing to study spiritual healing. I was convinced I would be a better nurse by preventing, and teaching prevention of, disease—and how to avoid hospitals. Again I am reaching the same conclusion in my heart. I feel the highest thing I can contribute may be to help prevent the Birth Trauma. To that purpose I dedicate this book. I want to heal all of us with the words that come to me here in the presence of the Master.

I am thrilled to think of a baby's being born who had little or no Birth Trauma. Dr. Leboyer's research has already proved that babies born with the quiet birth are brighter, healthier, happier—even ambidextrous—and more joyful. Who would not want this? What mother does not want to imagine that she could have the whole childbirth experience without pain? We must start with the thought that this is possible. In GOD all things are possible.

When I first heard about the "Russian Method" of birth, where mothers delivered the baby right into water, it made total sense to me. The baby has already lived in fluid for nine months, so being gently expelled into a larger area of liquid before having to cope with the shocking change of atmosphere was, it seemed to me, a better way of coming out. I was intrigued. The word got around the rebirthing community quickly, and three brave rebirthers tried it in 1980:

1. Barbara in Campbell Hot Springs, California

2. Jia in San Diego, California
3. Rima Beth in Austin, Texas.

Rima will give you a first hand account of her baby's birth after I have outlined my current idea of an Ideal Birth. This book is filled with helpful hints that will make your pregnancy a lot easier, whether you do the Russian Method or not. I feel happy that I can share with you what I have learned so far.

NOTE:

I CANNOT STRESS ENOUGH THE IMPORTANCE OF LISTENING TO THE BABY AS TO HOW IT WOULD LIKE TO BE BORN, HOW IT WOULD LIKE TO HAVE THINGS BE, HOW IT WOULD LIKE TO GROW UP. AND EVEN WHEN IT WOULD LIKE TO COME OUT AT DELIVERY!

Always acknowledging the fact that the baby is completely connected to Infinite Intelligence, and may be a being more enlightened than yourself, will produce wonders. Of this I feel certain.

Part I

What It Was Like to Write This Book

I have never had such unusual experiences writing any previous book. The whole thing began the day I shaved my head in the Himalayas in a pledge to surrender to my Master guru Babaji. As I watched my long hair float down the Ganges River, I felt my scalp. It was a very eerie experience. I felt like a newborn. (Babaji had recommended that we keep our heads shaved for nine months for this ritualistic initiation. I began to see that this had something to do with processing out any prenatal trauma.) I decided that this was the day I should start a book on birth. I had thought about it before, but I never got started. I knew a lot about the subject. Even though I had never been pregnant, I did not disqualify myself as a writer on this subject because I had learned so much as a prenatal nurse, and especially as a rebirther. For eight years I had relived people's births with them through the process of rebirthing. I had to write about it—I was suddenly bursting with information.

Every day for about two hours I would sit by the Ganges and write. I had never attempted to write a manuscript in longhand before. It seemed very laborious. I sat there in the Himalayan foothills, under an ancient tree on a tiny island in the middle of the Ganges River. It was an extremely holy tree. The vibes seemed to work for me. Writing about birth there brought up suppressed emotional birth feelings for me, which were readily available to me after years of rebirthing. (I was also fairly freaked out about my head shave and what that would be like for nine months in America!)

I began going into the cave where Babaji materialized his body to meditate. But the energy was so intense I could only take it every other day. I would crawl back in there to cry and breathe and curl up in the fetal position. I became a fetus in there, a baby, barely born. Often I would literally crawl out of there, shaken. A very old saint who guards the cave would come in and take care of me whenever I needed him. I would not have to call, he would just show up. He was more than my prenatal nurse—he healed me with chants and prayers, by rubbing herbs on me, massaging me, rebirthing me, holding me. I could never understand one word he said to me. He spoke only Hindi.

About my fifth session in the cave I went into a major spontaneous rebirthing. I had an intense past-life memory of a time I had had a baby inside that died and no one could get it out. I remembered the decisions I made, the feelings, the horror. Again the old Saint came in to take care of me. After this particular session, however, I was completely disorientated. I crawled out of the cave and onto the walk, pulling on the pant leg of a German devotee, begging him to help me across the river, up the 108 steps, and to my bunk. He obliged. Later, when my friend Phil came back to the warehouse where we were staying, he took one look at me and knew that my rebirthing was not complete. Being the good rebirther that he is, Phil took over. I had more energy in my body than I have ever experienced in my life. I told him about the past-life memory and he said "Well, I am not surprised. You have been working on that book for two weeks now." Had it been that long? I couldn't believe it.

Where *was* that book? I couldn't see my manuscript anywhere. It was missing! For two days I looked everywhere, and many others at the ashram helped me look for it. It was not to be found. I cried. I couldn't believe it. I took a long walk alone by the river and then I prayed to Babaji, telling him that I would go back to my commitment—I would do it over if it was not right. Perhaps *that* was the message. Something had been "off" about it. I let go of it. I committed myself to going to London and starting all over. But then I made one last prayer. I told Babaji if it was off in any way, he should keep it, I didn't want it back. But if it was correct, then *I wanted it back!*

That night in the temple, when I bowed before him for Darshan, I was trembling. But I told him anyway. I said "Babaji, I lost my manuscript." (As if he did not know.) I

3

was extremely embarrassed to call attention to this. He did not say a word. Finally he leaned over and looked me right in the face and asked "Why are you so careless?" I didn't know the answer, but I knew it was the right question. Then he said, as if taking pity on me "Well, I will put out a search warrant for it."

The next day a devotee came to me saying "I think I know where it could be." I said "Where? I have looked everywhere." But not this place . . . He told me that he thought it might be in the priests' quarters. I had never seen or heard of the priests' quarters. He led me to the tiny room above the cave. There it was, perfectly fine, in my black bag, guarded with all the other holiest objects. I cried. A few hours later I was heading back to the U.S.

But that was not the only time this manuscript was mysteriously "lost," both original and copies. I finally sent a copy to Rima to guard, fortunately! I actually had to rely on her for it. I cannot explain this disappearing and reappearing, except that it may have been too soon for this book to come out. I had to wait until 1984.

Then came a period where we went through all the problems of a very new thing that was moving too fast. Underwater birth stirred up a lot of "stuff" that I was not prepared to handle. I decided to go through a cooling-off period about the whole thing. I backed off. After flying to Austin, Texas to interview Rima and Steve, it certainly thrilled me again, but it just didn't seem the time to write about it. Then it happened that my female spiritual teacher gave me the message from the Tibetan Masters about this. She begged me never to abandon the underwater birth project. I committed myself again.

And then my book *Celebration of Breath* came out. When I saw *that* "baby" in actuality, I was so happy I immediately went back to work on this book. The funny part about it was that I ended up writing some of the last parts at home in Iowa on my sister's kitchen table. I was born on that kitchen table. Was I born to write this book?

Still amazed that this book seemed to have its own mind, I

4

found myself finally completing the galley review my first night in New Zealand. I would be in New Zealand for only two days, with guest lectures in both Auckland and Wellington. How was I going to find time to visit Estelle Myers at the Dolphin Centre in the area to the north where most of the underwater births had occurred? There was only one solution: Rent a twin-engine plane for the afternoon and fly there and back before my lecture. It seemed impractical and was very expensive, but there was no time to worry about that. I knew I had to go, even if it meant having only one hour with Estelle.

That hour turned out to be miraculous. I was able to help Estelle move to the next level of her research and I was given the excellent manuscript by Barbara Keller of the United States on the scientific reasons why underwater birth is favorable. My mission was complete. We flew back over heavenly New Zealand just in time for my evening lecture.

I had needed to hear directly from Estelle the instructions she got from the dolphins. When she told me in person I knew it was real. I found it impressive that the dolphins gave her instructions ("babies should now be brought from the water of the womb by a gentle transition to the water of the world so as not to experience fear") on the very day that Jeremy Lighthouse became the first underwater baby to be born in the U.S.

To the dolphins I want to say thank you. Please continue to teach us about peace, freedom and immortality. I would like to hear more from you.

Conscious Conception

The Ideal Birth begins with perfecting the conception.

Five years ago Leonard Orr said the following to me (after one year of rebirthing, when I was bragging that I could go into the water and breathe for an hour in the presence of another rebirther without anything coming up): "You think you are so smart, eh? Just wait until you get to your Conception Trauma."

I thought he must be crazy—me, remember conception? It had to be a joke. I couldn't believe it. Only two days later, I believed it. While having breakfast with a friend on Geary Street in San Francisco, listening to him talk about how the soul enters the body and choses its parents, I suddenly had my head in my plate and was rebirthing myself on the spot. I was astonished to remember my own conception. I came home and looked at Leonard. He laughed. We did not need to say a thing. He knew I knew.

The Conception Trauma involves this: Under what idea were you conceived? What was going on in the minds of your parents at the moment of conception and how does that affect you?

The conception "trauma" involves not only your parents' thoughts in the moment, but also their motives for wanting you. Also, were you wanted and planned by both?

- Did they have you to avoid the draft?
- Did they have you to save the marriage?
- Did one parent have any covert motive like: If I have a baby, maybe he'll stay home" or "If I have a baby, he'll change" or "If we have a baby she'll stop looking at other men," etc.
- Were your parents drunk or drugged at your conception?

- Were you conceived during intense marital stress?
- Were your parents healthy emotionally and physically at your birth?

This is fascinating research as a rebirther. Besides myself, I have had many clients remember conception. This also often happens in the presence of a true Master, who can process all your karma. What are *you* going to have in your mind at the moment you conceive a child? Think about this carefully. Think how wonderful it would be if your baby would be conceived in the space of total acceptance, total readiness, unconditional love and spiritual surrender!

I have rebirthed many hundreds of people where the situation was that one or both of the parents did not really want this baby. (Of course, on some level they did, since the baby arrived.) But the parts of the parents' minds that did not accept this birth affected these people's lives tremendously. The person often grew up feeling unwanted, and the anger and sadness about this (mostly suppressed) was immense.

I recall, in contrast, a woman I rebirthed who became a successful, enlightened physician. She was not only completely wanted; her mother actually had asked Jesus to pick the perfect soul for her to bring in and to pick the sex, promising she would accept it completely on faith. This being Judith, who is a friend of mine, is one of the most beautiful, joyful souls I know. Now, fortunately, she is involved in New Age birth methods of delivery. Thank you, God.

I feel the conception would be very enhanced were it ceremonial. Imagine welcoming a being in by making every attempt to bring it in through a most sacred experience. There could be not only candlelight, incense, tapes of chanting and/or joyous music, where lovemaking is Communion; but also any other sacred ritual that enhances the experience.

New Age Children

(This was summarized from the Spiritual Community Guide No. 4, 1978, *which is now published as the* New Consciousness Sourcebook *by Arc Line Publications, Box 1067, Berkeley, CA 94701, 415-644-3229.)*

The higher the couple's consciousness can merge during conception, the nobler shall be the incoming soul. Remember, the incoming child also choses parents, heredity, the karma it will carry, and its path. A matrix of perfection, like that which is found in a flawless diamond, must be held for your conceived child. Your responsibility as a parent of a child master is to be as conscious of loving as possible. Magnetize your own God Presence. To be a New Age parent, spiritual experiences must be protected so that the child can maintain its Godhood.

The Aquarian Age is bringing forth many child masters. There is a new cycle present in the last 25 years of the century enabling the collective vibrations of consciousness to be raised sufficiently so that many children can be born who are not ordinary infants. They are coming to set into motion a state of love and peace on the Earth plane. They are enlightened teachers and avatars with the potential for attaining Christ Consciousness. We must be prepared for them.

Scientists Talk About Conscious Conception

Writing in the *Brain-Mind Bulletin*, Dr. Stanislav Grof points out that "when a woman conceives a child she unconsciously experiences the cellular memory of her own conception." Memories can be negotiated. If you consciously reconstruct and complete your experience of physical trauma, you can be rid of its psychological effects. (This of course is one of the purposes of rebirthing.)

Therapists Mehl, Downing, and McNaughton stress the importance of "conscious gestation," in which parents communicate directly with the fetus. The fetus should be reassured of parental love, respect and joyful anticipation of its birth. The pregnant woman also can provide specific communications. If she becomes upset with her partner, for example, she can assure her unborn child, "It's all right, I am not mad at you and I forgive your father."

The article also makes it clear that birth and intrauterine experiences that threaten a baby's well-being persist in memory: In fact, they can have a lasting influence. Professional sensitivity is also imperative. Physicians' attitudes toward childbirth must change. The view of birth as an EMERGENCY is reflected in the tendency to create complicated pregnancies and difficult births. David Chuck, a San Francisco gynecologist, writes in the *Brain-Mind Bulletin* that "a woman becomes increasingly hyper-suggestive as pregnancy progresses, and she receives many negative inputs from the medical systems."

Change in This Profession

I was pondering, after reading this, why the medical profession (which I was part of for years, and with which I will always be involved) might be resistant to change. Why are any of us resistant to change? After years of rebirthing, I have learned that change may be scary because our birth was a scary change (liquid to atmosphere/small space to large space, etc.). We went through a change then that was immense, and it hurt; it seemed that all hell broke loose while we were going through it. So, change may be associated with fear, pain, disappointment, near-death . . . you name it.

Therefore, I recommend that those of us in the medical professions and in childbirth education, and in rebirthing, hold the thought that "change is safe. I can change without pain. I can change without hurting others. I can change without getting hurt." Being clear on these affirmations enabled me to change my entire life safely. Don't we all need to be clear on these thoughts, so that we can go ahead and make the changes we know we need to make in this important work? The flow of change in birth has been started universally, by the Universe. Hadn't we better let go into it? What if you are somebody who can actually effect these changes? What if you are withholding what you know about improving the situation? What if you are blocking some of those changes that you know need to be made? What if you knew *your own child* would come out a thousand percent better by being born by new birthing methods? What if he or she would come out smarter, more alive, healthier, more loving, more peaceful, more joyous? Wouldn't you fight for change in birth practices then? Wouldn't you see how this would affect your child's future, and the future of the world?

Dr. Thomas Verny's
The Secret Life of the Unborn Child

Recent scientific discoveries have dramatically changed the way we think about childbearing. Medical research has directed our attention to the physical vulnerability of the fetus and the psychological needs of the newborn infant. Women are admonished to give up cigarettes and alcohol during pregnancy and new understandings about "bonding" are heightening our awareness of the importance of the moments immediately after birth.

But now Dr. Thomas Verny, an internationally acclaimed psychiatrist, has taken our understanding of the birth process one step further. Synthesizing all of the recent medical findings with his own pioneering research, Dr. Verny presents compelling evidence that a person's emotional, psychological, and intellectual development begins in the womb. In his book *The Secret Life of the Unborn Child,* (with John Kelly; New York: Dell, 1982), Dr. Verny makes the remarkable disclosure that from the sixth month of intrauterine life, the fetus is a feeling, experiencing being who responds to and is greatly influenced by its environment.

Based on years of research, this book advances the theory that the unborn child is a reacting being who, from the sixth month—and perhaps even earlier—leads an active emotional life. Contrary to the traditional notion of the fetus as a passive, mindless creature, *The Secret Life of the Unborn Child* demonstrates that the fetus can see, hear, experience, and, on a primitive level, even learn. It suggests further, that parents have greater influence over the unborn child than ever before imagined.

Evidence of Dr. Verny's prenatal research and startling discoveries is included throughout his remarkable book. Among the fascinating personal case studies described are accounts of famous musicians who find that they can play certain pieces sight unseen, only to discover that their mothers had played the same music repeatedly while pregnant, and the story of a young woman named Cheryl who insisted that her adoptive parents call her Eileen and then discovered that her natural mother, who she had never known, had named her Illeen.

Dr. Verny explains that his findings have a profound implication for parents. He demonstrates that whether a child becomes happy or sad, aggressive or meek, secure or anxiety-ridden in later life, depends in part on what messages the fetus received in the womb. The chief source of these messages is the mother, whose ambivalence or fear about childbearing can psychologically scar the unborn child. Dr. Verny asserts that the father can have a significant positive or negative influence on the child's development as well. The secure presence of a father who loves the mother and is eagerly awaiting the child's birth contributes tremendously to a healthy and uncomplicated birth.

The Secret Life of the Unborn Child has received international attention. Written with John Kelly, it is regarded not only as a major contribution to the fields of prenatal care and obstetrics, but also as a vital addition to our understanding of human development and consciousness. Harlie Aizley, in *Modern Psychoanalysis*, (No. 1, 1982), writes:

> *Verny's book takes us on a psychic journey into the depths of human development. He demonstrates, with passion, the unequivocal significance of intrauterine life by presenting the unborn child as a feeling, remembering and responding being. Verny's work is revolutionary in that it challenges all of our previous notions of intellectual and emotional development and introduces us to an, until now, seldom imagined alternative. The foundation of his work is simply, "What happened prior is it." From this premise we follow Verny through an extraordinary investigation of the child's life in utero.*

Verny's work . . . offers us the precious opportunity to at last confront the intersection of the psychological and physiological aspects of pregnancy in an attempt to aid in the development of the child prior to his/her actual birth. When considering the potential influence these discoveries may have on the understanding, and thus prevention, of such phenomena as miscarriages, infantile autism, and other birth or pre-birth related disorders, it is indeed justified to view Verny's work as revolutionary.

What the Mystic Schools Teach About Conscious Conception and Pregnancy

When I was studying family sociology in college, I often wondered what it would be like if people had to pass some kind of test before they were allowed to have children, or even marry. I wondered if this would help stop crime, child abuse and insanity. After all, we had to have a test to drive a car! The whole idea made sense to me and I began to study the Futurist Literature. But then I abandoned the idea because it seemed impossible to get people to agree.

Now years later I have come across a book that made me think of all this again. This book, called *Woman —Torch of the Future*, by Torkom Saraydarian (Sedona, AZ: Aquarian Educational Group, 1980), talked about woman being the "guardians of life" I felt very proud and happy to be a woman, and inspired to write some of the highlights of this work. First, I would personally like to acknowledge the author, master of much ancient wisdom, for putting down this information, which he learned from other cultures. It is time we recognize there are other cultures that exhibit successful marriages, happy homes, healthy and beautiful children and almost no divorce rate. Shouldn't we learn from them?

When, in the author's youth, he visited many esoteric centers, brotherhoods and communities, he found the leaders thinking about how to create new generations that would lead humanity to a new society. These teachers were pointing out that human beings pay more attention when they are buying a horse than when they are marrying. Of course we have to face the pain and suffering that are caused because of poor choices in marriage. In the cultures he studied, the elders took great care to investigate possible mates for their children. A research team would study any history of crime, insanity, or severe health problems. Attitudes, talents, cleanliness, and work habits were assessed. Parents and relatives would suggest that a child not marry a person if conditions were not favorable. He writes:

It seems to me that in certain conditions it is a crime to marry and have children. Those who are not able to meet the responsibilities of family life should not marry and have children. To marry and have children must be for those who are especially schooled and prepared for it, as a man is schooled and prepared to be a lawyer or doctor. In a few hundred years people will marry and have children only if they pass through certain tests and requirements dealing with their physical, emotional and spiritual natures, and only then with the permission of higher authorities, who at that time will be the great spiritual physicians, priests, who will also represent the law. The girls and boys who don't pass the investigation? Some dedicate themselves to God and enter convents and monasteries . . . others go to work in hospitals . . . others do more schooling.

The group of investigators would find out if a boy was:

- Healthy
- Loving and considerate
- Brave and courageous
- Patient
- Diligent
- Educated
- Skillful and generous
- Honored in society and without criminal records
- Full of various virtues
- Fearless

- Not using cigarettes or drugs
- Of high morals and honest

Girls were evaluated with similar thoroughness.

Marriage was considered a sacred friendship, meant to bring in advanced souls and to provide for them the best physical, emotional and mental equipment. Real marriage went beyond physical concerns. It was the synchronization or harmonization of the mental plane—the fusion of the two souls into one rhythm. It was considered the duty of the married couple to help each other so that the Divine Self in each could find a way to manifest itself. A very important key for a successful marriage and family was that of a service project for the couple. They had to have a goal in which together they united their hearts and souls. Daily worship and a planned procedure for meditation were emphasized.

The marriage ceremony was very elaborate and important. It was also repeated every third year on the anniversary. There was emphasis on gratitude, tolerance, patience, sacrificial service, courage, joy, and solemnity.

Choosing the Baby

Certain meditations were given to those who were going to have highly developed babies. It was taught that parents could draw in old souls or young souls. Old souls come to work as leaders, talents and geniuses to further evolution. If the couple desired to bring in an old soul, the couple had to focus their desires on higher planes through meditation, contemplation and visualization of great ideas. The couple had to be in tune with each other, like two musical instruments. The right sphere of attraction for old souls was great love, respect and admiration. Great souls are drawn to great beauty.

The author explained how our political and economic conditions can be affected because of the incoming advanced souls. If many advanced people consciously plan to invite certain souls into incarnation, they can definitely cause great

16

changes in life. Conscious conception is a social responsibility.

Throughout this book, I stress the importance of conscious conception. I repeatedly stress how important it is to be clear as possible *before* conception. After years of rebirthing, where I have taken people back to the memory of conception, I am more and more convinced of the importance of avoiding not only the birth trauma, but the conception trauma as well. There was a time when I did not believe one could remember one's conception! Now I have to laugh at my own ignorance. Just because one cannot consciously remember something does not mean it was not recorded, or not affecting one constantly. Just yesterday I rebirthed a woman whose whole life was stuck at her conception.

You may never have considered the fact that you chose your parents. When you do, a lot will clear up for you because you will no longer blame them. You will begin to realize that you selected those parents to come through to teach yourself some lesson or complete some karma. Did you ever stop to think that if you want to get pregnant now, a soul is also picking you? It is important to exercise right thought, right speech and clear thinking if you want to attract high souls. Older, higher souls reject parents who are involved in any harmful acts because they do not want to be burdened by the karma of harmful actions.

Pregnancy — The Mother To Be

The author stresses that the welfare of a family, group, nation and all of humanity depends on the *quality* of the mothers. The mother is the standard of our survival, creativity, success and joy. The greatest opportunity a mother has is when she is pregnant. She can impress on a child the kinds of emotions, thoughts and creative urges which contribute to the future of the child and of humanity. A newborn baby is the sum total of his past—the strivings and failures of all his previous lives, as well as influences gathered

17

throughout the ages from his relationships. But the mother's influences while the child is in the womb makes a difference as to whether he remains *at the effect of* his past or becomes *at cause of* his future. It is therefore important to avoid being emotionally upset, negative, destructive, depressed, fearful, irritated and full of hate during pregnancy.

A mother-to-be should be mentally creative, so that the seeds of her creative ability will be implanted in the child. It is suggested that she be:

- Surrounded with beauty: nature and stars
- Surrounded with music: inspirational, spiritual and uplifting music that is soft, melodious and of great harmony
- Able to have long hours by the rivers, oceans and forests, listening to the songs of nature
- Presented with stories of great heros
- Inspired in a religious sense with practical examples of forgiveness, love and charity
- Given the best foods available
- Visited by people who have high moral standards and are healthy and beautiful
- Protected from negative, painful or disturbing news
- Encouraged to do needlework, embroidery, painting, music and various arts
- Kept away from noise
- Living in abundance and financial security
- Prayerful and meditative

I suggest you study carefully pages 71 to 93 in the excellent chapter "The Mother to Be." In the cultures studied the parents or custodians of the pregnant woman did not want anything other than beauty, health and harmony to come in contact with her. Pregnancy was considered extremely sacred. It was well understood that the embryo needed the best possible nourishment from the mother and that food was not the only nourishment. This included aspiration, vision, joy, ecstasy, lofty thoughts, ideas, beauty and the arts. The pregnant woman was considered to be like a photographic camera, impressing on the etheric body of the child whatever she sees. Television, for example, with all its portrayal of crimes, ugly conversation, hatred, revenge and distortions would *not* be recommended. Great literature, music and beauty, prayers and meditations of gratitude would be constantly encouraged. A pregnant woman was strictly forbidden to come in contact with any mediums, magicians or lower psychics.

At the end of this chapter, the author states that he strongly believes that the foundation of the civilization and culture is the mother, and that in the near future special universities will be established to prepare girls for womanhood and motherhood. Of course it is true, and I strongly support the statement, that if people want a better world to live in, the greatest attention and care must be given to the pregnant woman.

Training the Child During Pregnancy

Touch the abdomen and say:
"Baby, listen very carefully, I your mother advise you to have a direction of beauty, goodness, and truth in your life . . . I want you to be really beautiful physically, emotionally, mentally and spiritually.

"You must always try to be harmless, loving and helpful. You must be courageous and extremely fearless. You will not let other people misuse you.

"No matter what happens in your life you will never abandon your joy; you must always be joyful and always spread joy.

"You are going to be a really healthy baby and you will stay healthy. You will never catch cold and you will never be affected by disease. You will never get cancer. You will accept no sickness at all.

"You will try by all means to be truthful to your conscience, to God, and to the highest good and welfare of humanity.

"You will be courageous and fearless and work for the construction of a new world.

"You will be creative and bring with you inspiration from the higher realms."

After the Birth

After the baby was born, there were guidelines for the mother to follow. Breastfeeding was carried on for two years, during which time the mother was careful not to have any emotional problems, anger, fear, irritation or hatred. If this was happening, breastfeeding was stopped. However, this was prevented by others' helping her calm down through advice, meditation, prayer, rest, walks in nature and reading of inspiring books. When the father came home, he would immediately shower and change into fresh clothes before visiting the wife and baby to avoid the shock of psychic emanations. The baby was not allowed to be held by anyone who was considered morally, spiritually, or physically unhealthy. Mothers were taught to avoid arguments and fights. Most of the new mothers had their own mothers with them to act as advisors.

Mothers were expected to teach the child:

- The value of life
- The beauty of life
- The unity of life

- Respect of life
- The enjoyment of life: enjoyment of serving, enjoyment of helping, enjoyment of creating
- Aspiration toward great achievements
- An attitude of gratitude

Mothers were expected to be an example of honesty, goodness and beauty. They were taught never to condemn, criticize, or threaten their children, but rather to understand, explain and enlighten them.

A baby was considered to be a rare flower that must be raised in the right conditions. A sage told the author that the supreme thing a mother must give her child is noble character. This can be done when the mother brings into action the spiritual aspect of the child and kindles beauty, generosity, simplicity, dignity, strength and compassion (Babaji would say "truth, simplicity, love and affection.") The character of the child is first built by the example of the mother. A child cannot *be* through what the mother *says*, but what the mother *is!*

Controlling children by hate or bribery, the author warns, is the most dangerous technique. It either paralyzes the child or makes him an outlaw. Parents in the cultures studied were taught not to argue, fight, or display disrespectful manners in front of the children. Criticism was forbidden, ugly jokes between husband and wife were forbidden. Anger and hatred were also very much controlled in the presence of children. The parents were expected to be very honest with their children. Appreciation was expressed to the children. Before age fourteen all children had information about sex.

At the end of this chapter the author discusses the issue of negative influences of TV and bad literature. He says "Until dedicated teachers and parents protect their students and children from the pollution of TV, movies, bad literature, and other distructive influences we will never have a better generation. It is of no use to tell children not to kill when 24 hours a day they can see crimes and legalized war on TV.

How can we teach a child to love when hate is advertised day and night? The children of the New Age must develop a courageous spirit to clean the planet and humanity from all destructive activities for the sake of one humanity."

It was the father's duty to:

- Take his child out into nature
- Raise the child spiritually, teaching the laws of karma
- Prepare himself by being healthy, emotionally mature, financially sound, to master the art of communication
- Set an example and be creative

Education

It was well understood that one could teach a child even before he was born in these cultures (see also *The Secret Life of the Unborn Child*, by Thomas Verny and John Kelly—see p. 11 here).

It was believed that before a child was exposed to religion, he must have a trained mind in order not to fall into traps, so that he could eventually analyze, discriminate and choose his own religion with his own free will. It was believed that religious doctrines and Bible study would precondition the child's mind to such a degree that he would not be able to free himself from the limitation of the doctrines, dogmas and traditional influences. It was felt there was a danger of brainwashing. Children were instead given the essence of the religions without separatism.

Women—The Torch Bearers

The author beautifully summarizes the role of woman, not only in family, but also in the world:

- To protect life
- To protect the right development of life

- To evoke the highest talent in man
- To protect beauty
- To protect peace and harmony
- To protect the age long fruits of the labor of humanity
- To protect the teaching from degeneration
- To encourage the best in all fields
- To strive towards the future
- To learn and teach the laws of sacrifice and service
- To produce the highest survival techniques
- To inspire creativity in all fields
- To reveal the future possibilities of life
- To explain the law of love and compassion

The New Age woman will teach the value of life, he stated.

I salute you, Torkom Saraydarian. As a woman, I am happy to accept this responsibility. That is why I wrote this book.

Education Begins Before Birth

(This chapter is a summary of the important book Education Begins Before Birth, *[Los Angeles: Prosveta, USA, 1982.], written by the Master Omraam Mikhael Aivanhov, who brought the teachings of the Great White Brotherhood to France, where he has lived and taught ever since.)*

In this beautiful writing Aivanhov talks about the highest possibilities for yourself and your child. The best way to prepare yourself for parenthood is to realize that it is you who attract your children to you before conception. Why not consciously try to attract divine beings, geniuses, into your family? The best way to do that is to make sure that your thoughts and feelings, indeed your whole attitude and way of life, are such as to attract exceptional beings. Yes, this is possible, he insists. This notion is in complete alignment with the principles of *Ideal Birth*. In fact, it is one of the foundations on which this book is built. Most people don't even know the tremendous power they have in *choosing* their children *before conception*. If they did, they would surely prepare themselves for months or even years before conceiving a child!

Aivanhov reminds us that this is a sacred act. Are you prepared for a sacred act? Are you healthy? Do you have the means to provide for a child properly? Do you have the qualities you need to be a constant example? Do you have the ability to give your children security and consolation at all times? Are you ready to be a good parent?

What if you pick a moment to conceive when you are loaded with alcohol and not fully conscious of what you are doing? What if you are just in poor condition at the moment of conception, mentally, physically or emotionally? What elements do you suppose are introduced into a child under these conditions? Mikhael Aivanhov inspires you to *wake up* about this.

Do you want to have a wonderful experience raising a child? Well, then, you must know that a conscious conception is very important. Aivanhov also points out that if parents are fighting, cheating and being discordant, a baby in the womb can become nervous and ill. The baby is extremely receptive and its etheric body feels shock. For further well-documented research on this, again I recommend *The Secret Life of the Unborn child,* (see p. 11 here for the reference.)

Aivanhov reminds everyone that, to have the right to invite spiritual entities into your aura to incarnate as your children, you must be fitted for the task. If you really want to be a loving parent you must start correcting attitudes that could have a bad effect on your child. The point is that parents can be instrumental in determining what kind of person their future child will be. Superior beings will only agree to incarnate with parents who have already achieved a certain degree of purity and self-control.

The conception of a child should not be left to *chance.* (This is sinking *low* as a human, he points out.) Rather, it is something for which parents should call on Heaven, asking the angels to come and help them to attract a powerful, luminous being into their family.

He states that you can make your children of gold instead of lead. This process Aivanhov calls "spiritual gold-plating." (The quality of the seed which a man gives to his wife at conception depends on his degree of evolution. During the nine months of gestation the mother supplies all the materials needed to carry out the program. She influences the seed provided by the father by giving it conditions that will either enhance or detract from the child's characteristics. She must watch over her feelings and the kind of life she leads.) Aivanhov writes:

> As soon as a woman is pregnant a current begins to flow between her brain (the anode) and the seed. The brain receives energy from the battery God, the foun-

*tainhead of cosmic energy to which it is connected, and
this energy flows from the brain to the embryo. The solution is the mother's blood in which both anode and
cathode, the brain and the uterus, are immersed. (p. 27)*

The main point to get about this spiritual gold-plating, is that
it is imperative that the pregnant woman harbor only luminous thoughts during this time—thoughts that are positive,
loving, light, productive and spiritual. A mother can produce great miracles since she holds the key to the forces of
life. His mother, while Aivanhov was in her womb, conse-
crated him to God's service.

Waiting until a child is born to take it to people to instruct
it and educate it, is *too late*, he states. The die has already
been cast.

After years of rebirthing people and getting rebirthed myself, I have been shown with certainty, that what he says is
true. Bonding with your baby before conception, and *in
utero*, can make all the difference in the world!

I agree with this author when he makes a plea to all of us
to get our priorities straight. Why spend billions on hospitals, prisons, law courts and schools when, if we would focus
attention on our pregnant mothers, we might not have to?

"The future of the human race is in the hands of our pregnant women."

He recommends there be places where pregnant women
could go that contain perfect vibrations. Ultimately, the
whole period of pregnancy should be spent in a beautiful
poetic atmosphere where the parents could read, go for
walks and listen to music. Ideally, there would be lectures on
how to live and think during gestation, special nutrition instructions, and especially a place for "mental work."

He talks about breastfeeding and how important it is for a
new mother to take care not to give the baby the breast when
she is angry or in a negative frame of mind. Her negative vibrations actually poison her mind, and the baby could receive elements that might make it physically or psychically
sick. A nursing mother should always give her baby *con-*

scious attention during this time. She should think of it, talk to it, and give it her heart and soul. (If you are a nursing mother, or about to be, remember this.)

The Spiritual State of Mind Necessary To Be a Good Parent

It would not be admirable, he points out, to be so attached to the child that your reationship with God is neglected. If you neglect spiritual life to devote yourself to the child, you deprive him of the divine life, which is the only true life. this cuts the child off from beauty and harmony, and puts him in danger. Aivanhov bluntly states that if a mother neglects God and thinks only of her child, whatever she gives her child will be *lifeless.* This kind of affirmation-prayer would be appropriate instead:

> *Lord, I turn to Thee for light, love, health and all the beauty of Heaven for my baby.*

A mother should never do anything for her baby without first turning to God to draw that which she can then communicate to her child. This guidance could entail leaving the children now and then to improve your mind. You can't be so attached to your child that you would be afraid to leave it with someone while you went to purify yourself and receive spiritual guidance.

The author points out that as long as mothers make no effort to reach out to the highest levels of light, purity and eternity, their children will receive only the most ordinary elements from them. Do you want a child who is capable of doing wonders for society and humanity? You must, then, add elements from another dimension to produce this divinity. These elements can only be found in the spiritual dimension.

An example of how to do this:

> *A few minutes a day during the pregnancy, and later as the child grows, lift your thoughts to God, saying "I*

want this child you have given me to be Your true servant. I beg You to give me all the sublime elements which only You can provide, so that I can give them to him."

Pre-conception Preparation
of Parents

It would be ideal, of course, for both parents to be as enlightened as possible before conception of their baby. This would not only enable them to attract a more enlightened soul, but also everyone involved would benefit.

Child raising would be simpler and the result would be a much greater chance for the growth and development of a perfect, beautiful person who becomes a sheer delight and a citizen in the highest order—and who could make incredible contributions to the world. Therefore I recommend that future parents consider the following.

- *Rebirthing* (as mentioned—see Appendix)
- The *Loving Relationships Training,* or LRT (see Appendix). Obviously, if a child grows up with both parents, who continue to have a great relationship, this could change the world fast.
- *The Advanced LRT* (see Appendix). More personal case clearing directly on the subject of relationships.
- *Rolfing Deep Tissue Body Work and Other Body Work.* Having had, for example, ten sessions of Rolfing chances are much better (in my opinion) that the mother will have a much easier time in delivery, when the pelvic bones are lined up perfectly. I imagine it would help create a stronger, healthier baby with a more perfect body if both parents were "clear" on their own bodies. This is made easier with body work. Other trainings I can personally recommend include est and Actualizations.

Recommended Reading List:
- *I Deserve Love* (Ray)
- *Rebirthing in the New Age* (Orr and Ray)

29

- *Loving Relationships* (Ray)
- *The Only Diet There Is* (Ray)
- *Celebration of Breath* (Ray)
- *From Here to Greater Happiness* (Teutsch)
- *Life and Teaching of the Masters* (Spalding)
- *A Course in Miracles (Foundation for Inner Peace)*
- *Science of Everlasting Life* (Leonard Orr)
- *Spiritual Psychology* (Jim Morningstar)
- *Money Is My Friend* (Phil Laut)
- *The Secret Life of the Unborn Child* (Verny)
- *Birth Without Violence* (Frederick Leboyer)
- *Loving Hands* (Frederick Leboyer)
- *Birth Reborn* (Odent)
- *The Magical Child* (Joseph Chilton Pearce)

Also See Reading List in Appendix

Other Recommendations:
- Affirmations
- Prayer
- The Forgiveness Diet

Preparation for Pregnancy and Birth (Do with Partner if Possible)

1. List your ten greatest fears about pregnancy. Share them with your partner. Ask your partner to do the same and share them with you.

2. List your ten greatest fears about childbirth and share.

3. List your ten greatest fears about caring for an infant and share.

4. List your ten greatest fears about raising children and share.

5. Find out as much as you can about your own birth and the people that delivered you. Discuss it with your midwife and doctor.

6. List the things you love about being pregnant. Add to your list on a weekly basis, or whenever you feel like it.

7. List things you look forward to regarding your upcoming birth and your new baby. Share them, and add to your list regularly.

8. Clean up your relationship with your partner. Share the things you have been afraid to tell each other. Take turns. Acknowledge something you love about your partner after each sharing. Ask for support when you need it. Practice communicating your needs to each other.

9. Clear up relationships with your own parents.

10. Do affirmations regularly.

From:
Ananda Zaren
   Certified Birth Educator
   1709 Loma Street
   Santa Barbara, California 93103

Getting Clear on the "Five Biggies" Before Conception

Thanks to Leonard Orr, who coined the term the "five biggies," you can get clear in your consciousness beyond your fondest dreams. He said that the five most negative consciousness factors are these:

1. The Birth Trauma
2. The Parental Disapproval Syndrome
3. Specific Negatives
4. The Unconscious Death Urge
5. Other Lifetimes

These five biggies affect most people and keep them from experiencing bliss.

The Birth Trauma

The Birth Trauma includes all the negative shocks accumulated at birth—physical, psychological and emotional—leading to negative decisions which affect our whole life. A great percentage of our fear originated at our birth and it was often the beginning of THE UNIVERSE IS AGAINST ME Syndrome.

The advantages of getting your own Birth Trauma out of the body before conception and pregnancy are that the:

1. Baby develops in a mother's body where there is little or no fear, and hence has a chance to grow up without a lot of fear recorded in cells.

2. Baby has chance of a lot more aliveness.

3. Baby has less chance of picking up negative thoughts transferred from mother's and father's unconscious programming.

4. Baby has a better chance of becoming more beautiful after parents have breathed out "ugly" thoughts.

5. Mother has a better chance of happier pregnancy all around if she is breathing more and letting go.

6. Baby has chance of being a lot healthier, since the mother is breathing more oxygen.

7. Chances are of much less tension for everyone.

8. Delivery should be a lot easier because the mother can rebirth herself through it, the pelvic region will be more relaxed, and less fear in the mother during delivery will always make it easier.

See information on Rebirthing for clearing Birth Trauma.

Parental Disapproval Syndrome

The Parental Disapproval Syndrome develops as a result of parents having experienced disapproval when they were young and their consequent desire to get even, which they take out on their own children and mates. This syndrome is carried on from generation to generation and tends to destroy self-esteem. It is about how parents invalidate their children in the same way they were invalidated.

How It Could Affect the Baby

When the baby grows up in an atmosphere of total approval, it will feel unconditional love and will be a joy to live with. It will obviously be more cooperative.

Our research has shown that children do not need a lot of discipline. (They definitely do not need a lot of disapproval.) What they do need is a good example. Just as heavy disapproval can destroy self-esteem a lot of approval will promote self-esteem. Just as heavy disapproval is likely to bring rebellion, approval is likely to bring cooperation and harmony.

When new parents have completely forgiven their own parents, little or no suppressed resentment will be projected onto the children and therefore they will not have to fight back. The Forgiveness Diet is highly recommended prior to having a baby. (See *The Only Diet There Is.* [Berkeley: Celestial Arts, 1981].) The Loving Relationships Training is a quick and effective way to handle this syndrome.

The Unconscious Death Urge

The Unconscious Death Urge is all your programming and beliefs about death. It is the belief that DEATH IS INEVITABLE. This thought causes not only death, but also weakness and illness leading to death. It comes from the incorrect thought that there is a Source outside of you that can kill you.

People we have rebirthed who were born before, during, or after a death in the family, often suffered by coming into these vibrations. Coming into any situation where family members are preoccupied with death—unconsciously wishing it, programming for it, or recovering from a death, are all equally difficult for a new life. Our research makes it seem likely that many crib deaths could be explained as a result of the death vibe being too heavy in the atmosphere for the new being to tolerate. The soul simply leaves. This is where the child could become a sacrificial lamb, acting out the parent's own unconscious death wish.

Imagine the difference in a baby born to parents who had worked out their unconscious death urge and were aware of Immortality. The baby's aliveness quotient would be tremendous to start with. This alone could make the baby so healthy that it might never have disease. If it did, healing would be natural and swift. Imagine a baby completely healthy, happy, joyous and full of aliveness throughout childhood and all of life.

Specific Negatives

Specific Negatives are all your favorite negative thoughts that you use to beat yourself up. For example:

- I'm no good.
- I can't make it.
- I'm a failure.
- I can't do it.
- I'm not good enough.

The problem is that, whatever you believe to be true, you create. So if you have the thought "I'm not good enough," you will tend unconsciously to set up difficult situations to prove you are not good enough.

If future parents had released or resolved their most negative thoughts about themselves, the baby would be spared unconsciously copying them. They would obviously imbue the baby with more certainty and build in him a tremendous success consciousness. Imagine a growing baby where the parents have suppressed negative thoughts like these from their own birth:

- I'm not good enough.
- I can't trust people.
- I'm guilty.
- I'm unsafe.

Now imagine a baby whose parents did not have those thoughts, but had cleared them out and replaced them with these:

- I am wonderful.
- I am innocent.

- I love myself completely.
- I am trustworthy and so are others.

Every negative thought is a drain on energy.

Other Lifetimes

Other Lifetimes sometimes exert a strongly negative influence on our present lives. You can clear this up with specialists in past life regressions if you need extra help. We have found, however, that if you clear up everything in this life right down to conception, it will generally free you from any karma you may have been worried about. It is possible to remember even conception during rebirthing.

In other words, since your "birth script" is connected to your past lives, clearing your birth will release the chain. Therefore we do not spend a lot of time with past life regressions. However, occasionally there is something very "stuck," and then we would refer the person to a past-life counselor or other Spiritual Master. However, on many occasions people spontaneously remember past lives during a rebirthing session.

Discovering You Are
Actually Pregnant

When it is announced that you are pregnant, or when you intuitively know you are, CELEBRATION IS IN ORDER!

The fetus is just like an organ of your body. It responds to joy just as your heart, your stomach, or any other part of your body responds to your mental state. It probably responds a lot more to your mental state than anything. Joy is in order, no matter what is going on in your life. Any unpleasant condition cannot be as important as this new life coming in. So regarding anything concerning you, it is important to have the highest thoughts possible. For example, if you are stressed, trying saying:

I could see Peace instead of this.

Begin to watch every thought that crosses your mind. Raise the quality of your thoughts. Change any negative or limiting thought immediately to an affirmation. (See *I Deserve Love.*)

Begin every day with gratitude and celebration. Your growing baby will flourish wonderfully in this environment. This also applies to the father and those nearby, for a fetus can and does psychically pick up the vibes of those around it.

I recommend that both parents begin to communicate with the coming baby immediately and daily. Speak to it as if it were an adult (which it is, in a small body—a fully developed consciousness is coming in). The baby is already totally connected to Infinite Intelligence and can understand. It can feel and think in the womb. (We have often had people in rebirthing sessions remember during the pregnancy what the parents were feeling and thinking, and this was later confirmed by parents themselves.)

Therefore, it is of utmost importance that you as parents maintain an atmosphere of happiness, peace, joy and celebration during the pregnancy. (This does not mean, however, that normal feelings should be "stuffed" or "suppressed".) It is obvious that there may be fears and emotional mood changes. These changes should be expressed, not suppressed. It may be a very good idea for every pregnant woman to have a counselor, rebirther, or prenatal nurse to confide in. It would be ideal for this person to have continuous contact throughout the pregnancy.

A couple should have a "sharing time" daily in which each can feel safe to express all fears and doubts and feelings to each other without judgment. One partner talks, the other listens, then they reverse. The rest of the day is devoted to surrendering to the experience as much as possible. For the woman it is a time to let herself be as beautiful as possible, and as happy as possible.

Prenatal Care

I recommend that both the father and the rebirther/counselor be involved in all prenatal care. When I was running a Prenatal Clinic, I always enjoyed having the father in the room. It seemed much more complete and I was able to note the relationship and understand the family situation much better. If both parents are getting rebirthed, this would be an ideal setup to me.

Picking a Doctor or Midwife

This is of course a very personal decision. I would recommend that it be checked out as to which obstetricians or midwives are familiar with the Leboyer Method and the Russian Method of delivery. I would recommend interviewing several and finding one that you absolutely trust. This is the important thing, and it comes from following your intuition. Some obstetricans are getting very enlightened and getting rebirthed themselves. The obstetrician/midwife relation is very intimate with the future parents. If you are not satisfied, it is OK to change until you get what you want.

Inquire in your area about the following:
1. Alternative birth centers
2. Home birth by physicians
3. Lay midwifery
4. Alternative births in hospitals
5. Childbirth education classes.
6. For hospital, ask about rooming-in, birth rooms, Leboyer delivery, routine procedures, medication, and early discharge.
7. La Leche League (breastfeeding advice)

8. Rebirthing
9. Underwater birth
10. Spiritual counseling

Chiropractic and Maternity

by Michael Failla, D.C.
Seattle, Washington

If you haven't included chiropractic in your health maintenance program by now, then by all means this is the time to
do so.

In order to understand the benefits of chiropractic care it is
very important that you understand what health is. Health is
a condition of optimal spiritual, physical, mental and social
well-being. It is not just the absence of diseases and infirmi-
ties. It is much more than how you feel or even whether or
not you have a disease. It is a condition of wholeness in
which all the organs and systems both physical and non-phy-
sical are functioning at 100 percent all of the time. The key to
health therefore is function. The system responsible for function is the brain and nervous system whose purpose it is to
coordinate and control all of the organs, tissues, cells and
systems in the body and to relate the organism to its environment. When you interfere with the nervous system there is a
resultant loss of function and therefore loss of health.

Chiropractors recognize that health is the natural state of
being, assuming of course that there is no interference to its
expression. They realize that the body has its own capacity
to heal itself without the need of drugs as long as there is no
interference or damage to the body's communication system.

Nature needs no help—just no interference!

Chiropractors are experts in the art and science of locating
and removing vertibral subluxations, which are major inter-
ferences to your nervous system and therefore your health
potential.

A *vertebral subluxation* happens when a bone in your
spine moves out of its proper alignment with the other bones

in your spinal column or your skull or sacrum. When this happens there is a narrowing of the opening through which the nerves lie and also a narrowing of the neural canal through which the spinal cord passes. This causes an impingement; a pinching and irritation to the nerve or spinal cord and an interference with the communication messages (nerve impulses) sent between the brain and the body parts.

These communication messages or nerve impulses are really the energy (the spark of life) that the brain sends to all of the body's parts and organs to cause them to function with 100 percent health and efficiency. These are the impulses which keep the cells of the pancreas healthy and secreting the insulin that your body needs to metabolize sugar. This is the spark of life that keeps your muscles toned, strong and coordinated. This is the communication system that carries the intelligence that coordinates all of the changes an expectant mother's body goes through so that she provides a safe, nurturing and healthy prenatal environment for her unborn child.

If you are pregnant, your nervous system is of the utmost importance to your health and to the health of your unborn child. It is so important that in fetal development the brain, spinal cord and spine which houses and protects it are the first structures to emerge from a generalized mass of cells. The unborn child from the very beginning senses and feels things in its body through its developing nervous system. Its nervous system experiences the universe, your body, your thoughts, your feelings and your general sense of well-being through its direct connections with your nervous system. In other words, your nervous system is the channel through which your unborn child feels, senses and stores information about itself and the universe in its body.

Everyone should be checked periodically by a chiropractor for vetebral subluxations. It is especially important for both your baby's health and your own health when you are pregnant.

Most spinal problems begin as birth trauma. Even in the most gentle of childbirths there is a significant amount of stress to the newborn's spine (especially the neck in normal presentations, and low back in breech births) which causes the newborn infant from the very beginning to suffer from vertebral subluxations. These should be corrected immediately after birth. This is one way that birth trauma is recorded in the infant's nervous system and body, therefore, it is important to remove the vertebral subluxations at once. If they are not removed they will only continue to get worse. The baby's spine will not develop to be strong and healthy as it was intended to by nature. Irritated nerves will cause muscle spasms along the spine which will cause abnormal curvatures and scoliosis to develop causing weaknesses which will be hard to correct in adulthood. Growing up with pinched nerves will cause various organs and muscles to develop weaknesses which will set the stage for degenerative changes and diseases later in life and cause weaknesses in the child's and later adult's immune system rendering them susceptable to viruses.

Carrying your child during pregnancy puts a tremendous amount of stress on your own spine and exaggerates your own spinal problems. Many women never experience back pain until they become pregnant and then they suffer with it daily and it even continues after the baby is born.

Women who are under regular chiropractic care during their pregnancy report far less back pain, nausea, headaches, and fatigue and are much more comfortable and healthy throughout their pregnancy.

Women who have gone into "back labor" (the experience of excruciatingly sharp back pain that shows up only during delivery) in previous births report that it didn't happen under chiropractic care. Back labor is virtually non-existent among women who are adjusted prior to delivery.

As the delivery day draws near be sure to be in close contact with your chiropractor and have him adjust you on a regular basis. As soon as you go into labor have your chiropractor examine you and adjust any misalignments. Your delivery will go much easier if you have 100 percent nerve energy flowing through your body. You will tire less easily,

43

have a lot more energy and your muscles will be stronger for pushing the baby out.

If you can, have your doctor of chiropractic present for the birth as it may help your delivery if you are adjusted during labor, especially if you have had chronic back problems, and then he can examine and adjust the baby shortly after delivery.

After the delivery your chiropractor will help you to get your spine realigned to its natural position quickly so that you can be totally there to comfort, nurture and bond with the new life entrusted in your care.

Other Suggestions for Good Prenatal Care

Nutrition

The obstetrician or midwife will give you a good diet. In addition, remember this: Eat what you feel good about. If you are nibbling on six chocolate bars and you know you don't feel good about that, take note: The guilt you would have afterwards puts a poison in your body that is worse, or at least just as bad, as the poison you think sugar has. Now you have two poisons.

Meals should be relaxing and pretty, colorful, and always joyous. Take time to chew your food slowly.

Worrying about getting fat creates more poison because worry is like poison to your body. Let go of it! Think about God instead. Do affirmations. You have a choice.

Either:

1. You can be constantly worried about gaining weight and how your body is "losing its shape" and secretly resenting the baby because you are "losing your figure," or

2. A milder form of the above, or

3. You can delight in the miracle of your body, that it can expand enough to allow another being to come in, and you can give thanks to God.

Which way will your thoughts go? You are in charge of your thoughts! (Read *The Only Diet There Is* [Berkeley: Celestial Arts, 1981] to get cleared of negative thoughts about food.)

Massage and Great Sex

My personal opinion, as a former prenatal nurse and current Rebirther, is that there should be *as much* of these *as possible*. Without guilt.

Communion with Nature

This is the time to go outdoors a lot and take walks. This is the time to be appreciative of the earth and love it dearly. This will help the infant to gain a very healthy outlook about the outside of the womb, where he will be living. This will also help the parents stay more connected to the Source and keep their minds clearer. Going to the beach, mountains or woods seem to me to be very important throughout pregnancy, whenever possible. I have also delighted in seeing families camp out with newborns when the weather is right. Obviously these things would be great to continue as often as possible in the early years of the child. The child will surely desire and delight in it, especially if the habit were begun when it was in the womb.

Meditation

Being alone in quiet with the baby and God during the pregnancy is one of the highest things one can do. If you have trouble calming the mind, you can simily chant mantras or affirmations until the mind is still enough to sit quietly. I would encourage both parents to meditate with the baby daily and begin to receive messages from it. During this time the parents can also use *visualization* to imagine the highest quality life for the baby, and the easiest birth.

Reading

Make a habit of reading uplifting, stimulating, affirmative books while pregnant. A list is provided in the back of this book.

Swimming During Pregnancy

Susan Schaffer writes in *Swim Swim* magazine that "swimming is often considered the best sport for pregnant women. The water supports the body weight, minimizes stress on the tissues and cools the swimmer as she exercises." Swimming, she says, also strengths the abdominal and back muscles, reducing the likelihood of backache in late pregnancy and enabling the mother to push harder during delivery.

By the fifth or sixth month, she suggests, the pregnant woman "needs to make some changes in her swimming style." For example, kicking can cause dizziness or faintness because blood from the legs is less efficiently returned to the heart. Face-down strokes could also become exhausting or painful. The backstroke is reported to be the easiest in late pregnancy. Pregnant women who swam during pregnancy could feel their unborn babies swimming along with them.

She recommends, of course, that your doctor or midwife have full knowledge of this. (As told in *Working Woman*, July 1983)

The Sex of the Child

The ideal birth is where the parents are thrilled with the sex of the child, no matter which it was! This is easy if you are willing to have God give you what is best for you.

I have seen a lot of damage done to a person's psyche because of the disappointment the newborn itself could feel when it came out (or earlier—in the womb). A baby senses and feels everything. It is completely telepathic and picks up all the energy around it like a sponge.

During rebirthing many people recall what their parents were thinking all through the pregnancy. This is stored in the subconscious. Often these clients recalled being aware in the womb that they were not wanted as the sex they were. This resulted in fear of coming out and complicated deliveries like breech (turning around because of not wanting to come out). It also resulted in overdue pregnancies.

Since we now know with certainty that babies make very sophisticated decisions at birth with which they have to live (and that these decisions create strange results in their lives, at least until they come to awareness), it is imperative to study some of those cases where a baby was a different sex than the parents wanted. This research continues.

The baby, who is completely tuned in to Infinite Intelligence and able to think, could decide the following:

"I am a disappointment."
"I'll *never* be good enough as a (female) (male)."
"I should become a different sex to please my parents" (homosexuality).
"I'm wrong."

Since THOUGHTS PRODUCE RESULTS and since WHAT WE BELIEVE TO BE TRUE, WE CREATE, a baby begins to set up his or her life accordingly. Obviously the child with conflicting thoughts will be more difficult to rear and will bring more heartache to the parents and to itself with the burden of these thoughts embedded in its soul.

Why not let God decide the sex of your child? It will be perfect for you, and imagine how great it all would be if you accepted it completely and unconditionally from the moment you knew you were pregnant!

Where To Have the Baby

Dr. Leboyer once said to me he hoped that we would one day work it out so that women had their babies at home naturally, just squatting down to deliver themselves. This is how the animals do it, and this is what I always saw in the Peace Corps in Peru. With the knowledge of how to handle one's mind and with adequate preparation, this makes total sense to me. Squatting down seems in harmony with gravity, as opposed to having the legs up in stirrups.

Now we are going a step further and developing the method of squatting down in the water and letting the baby come out into water. This is thrilling to me and I acknowledge my brave friends Rima and Steve and Mela for doing it. This book includes, in their own words, their direct experience.

There are now some very modern "birth rooms" of which I approve; they are located in medical facilities, but do not look "medical" at all. They are more like bed rooms with plants and soft lights, and the atmosphere is very homey. The medical equipment is all out of view.

Planning Ahead—
Who Is Present at the Birth

If the baby is born at home, there is a lot of room for choice. Since we are talking about the Ideal Birth, I will say that if everyone in the birth room had been rebirthed to completion, that would be my idea of the Ultimate. We begin with hoping that both parents have been fully rebirthed or released from the Birth Trauma. Next it is most advisable that the obstetrician or midwife be rebirthed. I hope this will be possible in every city in coming years. I recommend an article written by my friend Dr. Phil DuBois; see *Rebirthing in the New Age* (Berkeley: Celestial Arts, 1983).

If everyone in the room had been rebirthed, there would be little or no contamination of the psychic space. No one would be holding their breath during the actual delivery, which makes it harder on the mother and newborn to breath fully. (People tend to hold their breath in times of stress, just when breathing *more* would help reduce the stress. Holding the breath during emotional moments also keeps the energy "stuck.")

Everyone who has been rebirthed could more easily stay focused on loving the baby when it came out, rather than on their own fears. In general, if everyone were breathing deeply and connectedly (as people who have been rebirthed do, spontaneously), there would be less fear in the room. This would surely reduce the pain for the mother and the baby!

Make a list of those whom you would like present and prepare them. Reading this book would help them. People to share the birth might include:

1. Father
2. Midwife or doctor
3. Rebirther(s)

4. Friends
5. Photographer
6. Rolfer or chiropractor available
7. Relatives
8. Sensitives who enhance the energy, or Spirit Guides

Be aware of how many you can handle appropriately. All these people should be rebirthed and prepared.

Preparation of Siblings

I have rebirthed many people who were extremely affected by the birth of another child. They had not been adequately prepared for the arrival of a new sibling, and as a result they became very sad, angry and upset. In several cases, they never fully recovered from the jealousy and rejection. I have also rebirthed people who were on the other end: the newborn who came out feeling the resentment of the older sibling.

What can we do to reduce sibling rivalry? How do we honor birth, unite the family, and realize this is also a birth of a lifelong relationship between siblings?

At the Denver Birth Center, Loretta Ivory, a Certified Nurse Midwife, is experimenting with letting young children watch the birth of a sibling (*Life* magazine, July, 1982). Susan Riederer and her husband, Paul, began including Matthew in the new pregnancy immediately. (He counted exercises with his mom, she got him used to the noises of labor.) At the hospital he was completely caught up with excitement and burst into applause when the baby came out. The result was that he continued to make a big show of brotherly love at home.

The program, however, is not universally popular. Some people are scandalized by it, others intrigued. It is catching on, even so. Actually four hundred birth centers in hospitals are getting into it, plus hundreds of individual birth centers.

Try to imagine ways you could prepare siblings for this birth.

Suggestions

1. Talk to your other children about it *before conception.* Tell them all of your feelings and be totally honest. Do

not manipulate or begin to bribe them. Ask them to share any feelings they have.

2. Begin to show them books on the subject.

3. Have them help you pick out things for the new baby.

4. Have them help you select a name.

5. Do not assume that they will not understand, no matter what age they are. Talk to them about what it might be like.

6. Give them space frequently to share any jealousies, fears and feelings about this. Don't argue about it. Say "Thank you for telling me that. What else do you feel?"

7. Ask them what kind of relationship they would like to have with this being. Help them to imagine what they could do to create a really great relationship with this being who is coming.

8. Talk about sharing and the fun of sharing things.

9. See appropriate movies.

10. Make art for the baby's room.

11. Add your own ideas to this list.

Ways in Which I Could Prepare My Other Children for this Birth

1. _____
2. _____
3. _____
4. _____
5. _____
6. _____
7. _____
8. _____

9. _____

10. _____

11. _____

12. _____

The Question of Anesthesia

Excessive use of drugs is discouraged in labor and delivery. It is more scary for the newborn when the mother is not conscious. When the mother is drugged the tissue around the baby feels dead. (Brain-Mind Bulletin)

I have rebirthed many people who "remembered" that their mother felt dead. They had gone through tremendous fear thinking that they had killed their mothers. Some of them ended up with the thought "I'm a killer," formed just in that moment. Often the client's thoughts at that moment went something like this: "I am ready to live . . . they are killing me . . . I feel like stone . . . I am going out . . . fading . . . (rage) . . . there is nothing I can do . . . feeling unconscious."

Are we programming for a drug-dependent society by giving babies the cellular memory of countering stress with drugs?

In rebirthing we often have clients who "go out" during the rebirthing while the suppressed drugs (which had crossed the placenta) are coming out. These people are often in a "fog" their whole lives until they breathe out the drug in rebirthing. Often we can even smell the anesthesia in a rebirth.

The first scientific study of correlations between anaesthesia/birth injury and later emotional and physical distress was conducted by a Swedish medical doctor while doing research at the University of California at Los Angeles (UCLA). By examining the birth records of individuals who had become alcoholic, drug addicted, or suicidal, Dr. Bertil Jacobson discovered that these behavioral disturbances corresponded to the administration of tranquillizing barbituates to their mothers during labor. Jacobson suggests that at birth, babies have a heightened sensitivity to impressions and are somehow "marked" by these first impressions (reported by Elizabeth Grundstrom in "Anaesthesia Can Make Children Addicts." Stockholm: *Dagens Nyheter*, November 28, 1985).

Labor

Labor and delivery is a time when one has a greatly enhanced opportunity to master the mind. I think the most important things for making the experience easier are these:

1. Understanding the experience of doing connected breathing
2. Knowledge that you can instantly change each negative thought to the opposite, which will always reduce fear and pain
3. Faith (and a staff you trust)
4. Support from others
5. Making the space very comfortable and relaxing
6. Massage
7. Appropriate music
8. A place to walk
9. General attitude of calmness, affirmation, trust, and prayer
10. Other measures (Example: Women in some cultures belly danced to "bring down" the baby. This is how belly dancing originated.)

Without these things, the experience could be difficult and frightening. Taking time to experience them can make all the difference in the world!

A mother needs to remember that if she has a scary thought (like "I can't make it," "I can't do this," or "This is killing me,") she does have the opportunity in the next second to change the thought and take hold of her mind. Hanging on to scary thoughts could make labor very long and trying. There could be a lot of suffering. These kinds of thoughts are like the devil (Ego) and one almost has to say "Get thee behind me, Satan" and "I will not indulge in such thoughts." Change these thoughts immediately to:

"I can make it."

"I can breathe through this."

"I can transmute this energy into pleasure."

"I am safe. The more I remember I am safe, the more I can relax."

"I am letting go."

Any thought beginning with *I can't* will keep you stuck in hopelessness, helplessness and fear.

My mother tells me that when I was born (at home, on the kitchen table), she amused herself during labor by going in the other room to whistle whenever she felt a contraction. She said this worked very well. To this day when I hear someone whistle I am immediately in bliss—the bliss of the womb. Try *anything* not to "go into agreement with" the so-called pain. I object to the term *labor pains* and even to *contraction*. This sets up the mind to expect the worst. There must be a better word. How about *expansions?*

I would think one of the best ways to deal with this moment would be to do connected breathing and mantras. Chanting *Om Namaha Shivai*, or something similar, would surely bring more relaxation and ease.

Affirmations

- I am completely safe.
- I am completely safe in childbirth.
- Childbirth is a safe, natural happening.
- The more I give up my fear, the more relaxed I am and the less pain I have.
- Everything is happening quickly, which helps me to let go of my fear.
- I am safe in God.
- I am safe and immortal right now.
- I can easily allow these symptoms to be absorbed by the energy that makes my body feel good.
- I can feel good all during delivery.
- I let God manage all of the pregnancy, labor and delivery.
- I surrender completely to God.
- I allow this to be pleasurable because I am free of guilt and do not need to punish myself.
- I am innocent and my baby is innocent.
- My contractions are actually pleasant as long as I do not resist.
- I no longer resist.
- I do not resist God.
- I breathe fully and freely and let go.
- I am strong enough for this.
- I can transmute everything into love and pleasure.
- Childbirth brings more aliveness to me.

Start writing several of these affirmations a few times every day. You can use them at any time, and the earlier in the pregnancy you start them, the better the effect.

The Birth Itself

The best way I can write about the actual moment of birth is to describe one that is the most ideal I have heard of. This is told by the parents in Part III of this book, on underwater birth. It is extremely valuable to read this chapter even if you are one of those people who choose not to do underwater birth. This is because you will learn a great deal from reading about the attitudes the parents had during the pregnancy, how they prepared themselves for delivery, how they handled the delivery, and especially the mental state they had during labor and delivery that enabled them to have an ideal birth.

For the more technical aspects of delivery, I recommend studying the books of Sheila Kitzinger. Also, there is an excellent list of books in the Appendix.

I don't mean to imply that the only ideal birth is an underwater birth. Since this is not yet practical, we must see how we can make every birth ideal. I have asked Dr. Bill Hindle of Hawaii to address this subject.

The Miracle Before Birth

by William H. Hindle, M.D.

This chapter might well have been titled "The Miracle Before Breath." During the acute transition of birth, infants confront death and, with their own breath, establish living. Each breath thereafter is a renewal of the living forces within the infant physically, emotionally and spiritually.

The miracle of birth has been celebrated and documented through centuries. Only recently has the miracle before birth been scientifically verified. It is now known that infants before birth respond to sound, motion, stress and emotion—both their own and their mother's. Even in their physiologic protected environment, infants are sensitive and aware. One begins to establish behavior patterns and manifests biological rhythm within the womb. Life in the womb is a time of communication. The infant in the womb is probably unaware of its physiologic dependency which will be so overwhelmingly manifested after birth. The human infant is unique in its total dependence after birth.

Scientific studies have documented that during the second trimester of pregnancy, the infant becomes aware of its environment. The infant can see, hear, taste, learn, react, and experience. Emotional and physical life has begun. Patterns may be set at this time for behavior which will persist for the rest of that individual's life. There is evidence that the mother can consciously imprint the infant by her own behavior and emotional mind set. This is prebonding between mother and infant while still in the womb. In order to develop appropriately, infants require stimulation while within the womb or they can atrophy from neglect the same as infants after birth. In the womb, the infant is nurtured emotionally as well as physically. The intrauterine infant is imprinted by the intensity of feelings and constant/persistent maternal emotions. The documented effects of smoking and alcohol intake by the pregnant mother upon the fetus is conditioned not only pharmacologically but also by the emotional state of the mother. During development in the womb, an infant can adopt the maternal speech pattern which will not be evident until the child's verbal communication begins. Infant communication outward is limited, but seemingly the intake is extensive.

Normal heart rhythm (pulse rate) is soothing to the infant long after birth. Maternal positive attitude can provide an "intrauterine bonding." Even the father's pregnancy emotions can be transferred to the fetus as they affect the mother. An infant supplied with continuity of love by the mother can tolerate thoughts of rejection and negative emotional stress as long as these are not consistent maternal patterns. The mother functions as an active communication channel far more than a passive conduit to the unborn infant. Maternal rhythm of sleep habits and the quality of that rest emotionally and physically are transferred to the infant, which can predispose to either a healthy or abnormal sleep pattern for the child after birth.

Under hypnosis most women can visualize the sex of their unborn infant. Similarly maternal dreams are major methods of the mother's handling pregnancy emotions, especially the fears of an abnormal infant and a complicated labor and delivery.

The child in the womb knows what is going on around the warm liquid space in which it is collecting its first experiences and reactions. The personality of the unborn infant can be noticed in the activity and responsiveness of the infant within the womb. Regression therapy gives evidence that the intrauterine infant responds to the emotions of the mother, particularly if they are intense and persistent. From mid-intrauterine life, temperature and noise penetrate to the infant. The infant is seemingly unaware of what will happen at birth and thereafter.

Sight and thoughts are limited for the intrauterine infant but feelings, hearing, and emotions are responsive and well-developed. Communication of the unborn infant with the outside world is mostly by behavioral activity. There is no verbalization to get in the way of the infant's communicating to the outside world.

Cultural influences imprint on intrauterine infants as well. Society makes itself known before the first breath. Such gross physical actions as the traditional "kicking" can often be related to external environmental influences.

Continued input crosses from the mother to the fetus. Episodic, occasional influences, some of which may be intense, can be handled by the infant. It is the continuity of stimulation (positive or negative) that leaves the greatest imprint. Basic attitudes of the mother about herself and how she feels about motherhood, pregnancy and the infant are transferred to the developing infant in the womb. Tension, anxiety, fear, anger and hostility, particularly of high intensity and prolonged duration, have a negative impact. Feelings of relaxation, happiness, security and contentment supply a positive environment for the infant. The optimal conditions for the infant is that the mother hold pregnancy to be joyous and beautiful, something to be celebrated. In realtiy, the woman may watch the initial joy of the father contemplating proud fatherhood be replaced by resentment of the transformation of the mother's body into a form he finds less attractive. In fact, may women feel ambivalence and even self-contempt for the "ugly" body of pregnancy. Such feelings are normal if not dwelled upon persistently or intensely. Thus the maternal attitude is of critical importance in the emotional environment of the infant during pregnancy, as well as during labor and delivery.

Research has documented bonding before birth. The intrauterine child is perceptive to emotional environment and positive stimulation. In the womb this is nonvisual stimulation. The developing infant is sensitive to feelings, especially as perceived by touching and sounds. Hearing, feelings, taste, smell and sight are active within the womb, with resultant memory and learning. Behavioral studies have demonstrated mimickery after birth of behavioral imprinting during development in the womb. the balance of rewarding/punishing and pleasures/pain are operative in the intra-uterine environment. Even hugging, which develops into a basic supportive physical communication in later life, is imitated by physical actions, albeit done alone (by the infant within the womb). The seeming limitation of sight to about one foot immediately after birth may be a function of the limited "universe" the infant has had within the womb for the nine months prior to birth. There is an awareness of texture within the womb that immediately manifests itself in behavioral responses after birth. As in early childhood, the developing being within the womb responds to instant encouragement and reinforcement. This should be done within five seconds for optimum positive impact. The infant within the womb thrives on gentle movement—both its own and from without.

There *is* prenatal psychology, which is best nurtured by the sympathetic communication of a positive body image of the mother, a positive relationship of the mother with her spouse/partner, and a positive relationship of the pregnant mother with her mother.

The advice to pregnant women is to acknowledge the human being in the womb, be respectful of the aware and sensitive individual developing physically and emotionally within the womb, sympathetically communicate and, above all, enjoy.

Trusting in God During Delivery

The affirmation I like to give a woman for delivery is this: "My mind is God's Mind. I am one with God." What would God's mind be like? God is Eternal Bliss. His being is love, wisdom and joy. God would never worry. God does not create misery, pain, suffering, fear, guilt, anger, sickness or death. These mistaken creations are of the ego's thought system. We made up the ego. We made it up when we thought we separated ourselves from God. The ego is based on separation. As long as you think you are separate from God you will suffer guilt and fear punishment. One of the ways of punishing yourself is with pain. Pain is created by the ego mind. It is the effort involved in clinging to a negative thought. Because we have projected our ego onto God, we fear God. We have even gone so far as to make the mistake of thinking that God kills. This is insane. God is life itself.

Because we fear God, we do not feel safe with God, and therefore it is difficult to trust God. Yet God is the only safety there is, and trust would be instant if we did not confuse God with the ego. The ego is a collection of negative limiting thoughts we have made up that keep us from remembering that we are one with God. For example, thoughts like "I am bad" "I am not good enough" or "I am evil" could be buried in the subconscious, and these thoughts may very likely keep you from thinking you deserve to have a pleasurable childbirth free of pain. Or, if you had the thought 'I hurt my mother at my birth," you may simply assume you will be hurt in return. These thoughts are *in the way* of feeling trust and feeling God's love and safety. The most important thought to change during delivery is "Death is inevitable." How can you trust God if you think death is inevitable and that it could happen during delivery? How could you trust God if you think God causes death? Knowing that death is the result of a thought helps a lot, and knowing that you are in charge of your thoughts is the key. So you could just as easily have the thought "I am safe and immortal right now" or "God is my safety."

Focusing on the negative will increase pain and decrease trust. Why identify yourself with your weakness? Identify yourself with God. Do not hold a destructive thought. There is no need for a negative thought of any kind. Why not do chants during delivery? Have someone read the *Course in Miracles* to you out loud. You read it out loud. Do whatever helps you plunge your mind into the Infinite Thought of God. Talk to Him intimately. Breath in the Holy Spirit. Nobody can keep God away from you. God is there. You are one with God. You are not separate, but if you hold onto negative thoughts of any kind, you might not experience Him. Fear is a sign that you are not trusting and you are coming from separation. Trust is remembering who you are and that God's will is for you is perfect happiness, a perfect delivery of your baby.

Meditations for Trust During Delivery from A Course In Miracles Workbook

A Course in Miracles *is a three volume comprehensive spiritual teaching. Some people feel it is the most important writing in the English language since the translation of the Bible.*

The lesson titles from *A Course in Miracles*, as well as other material quoted from the course, are used by permission of the copyright owner, Foundation for Inner Peace, Box 635, Tiburon, CA 94920. The Course can be ordered directly from the Foundation for $40.00. It is also available in a paperback edition for $25.00.

Belly Dancing and Birth

Belly dancing is both ancient and female. It is a dance of body conditioning, natural childbirth and spiritual awareness. Mothers taught this movement form to their daughters as part of a cultural heritage which included Goddess worship, natural cycles and the physical strength, health and pride of women. Belly dancing has been, unfortunately, degraded and exploited by a patriarchal society.

In the ancient matriarchies, women were recognized as the creators of life and of culture. Birth was a sacred and celebrated event, to which children were invited and in which they often participated. The pregnant woman was attended by many sisters of every age, who danced around her and with her in rhythmic and circular patterns, helping her womb to open easily and naturally. The young women played musical instruments and imitated the undulating movements of the more experienced, and all the women joined together to witness this reaffirmation of their sexuality. These fertility rituals encouraged identification once more with the Goddess within.

Belly dancing came from *beledi* dancing, or native dancing. Because it is a birth dance, the name belly dance developed through the centuries to refer to the womb of women, the center of our creative life energies. Energy is channeled from the belly throughout the body in circular patterns and rhythmic impulses. The body's energy is constantly rejuvenated, as energy centers open gradually and harmoniously. The dancer experiences a sense of physical control and freedom that draws from intuitive and psychic sources. Such a vantage point allows for painless natural childbirth as well as disciplined bodily self-defense. And the body, being grounded in the trance like movements of the birth dance, frees the mind to travel and explore other realms of consciousness without fear.

Many of the exercises being learned today by women who wish a natural childbirth are akin to belly dancing. The undulations in belly dancing are movements corresponding to the second state of childbirth, when the mother begins to help the baby be born, working with the contractions and relaxing between, creatively merging and moving with the body's energies. The thrusts in belly dancing involve more staccatto and forceful energies. These correspond to the baby's attempt to assert its independence from the mother's womb. The "shimmies" correspond to the actual birth state. The motion is of high vibratory energy and expresses ecstasy. This builds up to the final vibratory birth reactions when new life enters the universe.

When Dr. Leboyer, who wrote *Birth Without Violence*, first came to visit the U.S., I hired a belly dancer to perform so that everyone could get in the mood. He was delighted, and it became obvious to everyone at the lecture what an addition this would be to any woman's labor.

How We Greet the Newborn, a Social Character

At the conference at Big Sur, California on "The Perinatal Period: Interface of Biology and Behavior," Susan Arms stated:

> *Immediate separation after delivery deprives both mother and child of their greatest opportunity for emotional bonding. This lack, when a baby is separated, undermines trust, and many babies spend the rest of their lives regaining trust.*
>
> *It is becoming quite clear that the manner in which a society greets its newborn members has a lot to do with shaping of its overall character. Much of our failure to develop peaceful behaviors in beings occurs during childbirth—due to lack of bonding and impersonal childbirth."* (Reported in Brain-Mind Bulletin, January 25, 1982)

As for me, on the day of my birth, there were many people around socializing and having fun, since I was born at home. My whole life has been very social; I have never had to work at making it that way. I feel very grateful for this. I can think of many things and experiences I would want at my birth if I were to be born as a baby again tomorrow. On the following page try making your own list of ways you could welcome and greet your new baby. I have listed some of my choices following your list.

Some Great Ways I Could Welcome My New Baby

(Remember that he or she is a conscious being, aware of everything, who feels and thinks.)

1. _____
2. _____
3. _____
4. _____
5. _____
6. _____
7. _____
8. _____
9. _____
10. _____

My Suggestions

1. Coming into lots of water and pleasure (underwater birth, or at least Leboyer bath).
2. Soft lights, warm room, music playing.
3. Chants and prayers.
4. Flowers and candles in pretty crystal holders.
5. Crystals.
6. Gifts beautifully wrapped.
7. Friends who are extremely loving, positive and breathing well—who understand the principles of this book.
8. The father and whoever the parents feel clear with.

9. Beautiful fabrics; much light and air in the room.

10. Periods of silence for receiving communication from the baby.

11. Spiritual teacher, spiritual healer, energy channel, and masseuse available; Rebirthers.

12. Atmosphere of celebration without raucous energy.

13. Siblings, well-prepared.

14. Gifts of money to develop immediate prosperity consciousness. (Remember, you can have gifts appropriate for all ages, since a baby is really many ages, many lifetimes, old.)

Immediately After the Birth

The first five minutes outside the womb is crucial. All Dr. Leboyer's research shows this. All of our research shows this. Freud suggested that we all got "messed up" in the first five years of our lives. Leboyer says "No, it is actually the first five minutes." (They call him the new Freud.) In Rebirthing, I was amazed to see how truthful this was. The "decisions" people had made in their first minutes were profound. Most of them negative—we call them Personal Laws. They are thoughts like these:

"I can't trust others."

"I'll never make it."

"People are out to get me."

"Life hurts."

"Life is a struggle."

"Life is a battle."

"I can't get what I want."

"The body causes pain."

"I'm not good enough."

"I cause others pain."

Since THOUGHTS ARE CREATIVE and THOUGHTS PRODUCE RESULTS, this is the way life gets created—from the first five minutes. As a Rebirther, it is imperative to know about this, helping the client to change his thoughts and breathe them out.

This is one of the main reasons I wanted to write this book. *Making the first five minutes out of the womb as perfect as possible is ALL IMPORTANT.*

Imagine making the first five minutes totally pleasurable. Coming out into water is one way. The baby, already familiar with water (amniotic fluid) is still in something familiar, just more spacious. There is time to adjust to the space before going on to the new experience of atmosphere.

The soft, gentle, lovely song called "Welcome to the World," which I included in my list of suggestions, was written by Marshall Summers. He wrote it for Frederick Leboyer in honor of newborns the night before Dr. Leboyer came to Theta House on his first trip to America.

I feel it would be a very sweet thing to play this record frequently to the baby at birth and for several weeks thereafter, throughout the first year, and later on.

It would be wonderful to have an atmosphere of Holy Celebration such as Jesus had when He arrived! Flowers, gifts and music are all appropriate. The baby registers all of this and will treasure it forever. The baby is aware of *everything*, and don't ever forget it.

Ideally, the baby should not be removed from its mother *for any reason* during the first week of life. Unless there is a dire emergency, which we intend to avoid by the procedures in this book, I cannot think of any reason good enough. I feel that I was very fortunate to be born at home and to have had this continuous bonding naturally. It has given me an attitude of trust, safety and nourishment. It is one of the things to which I attribute my success in the world, and I deeply acknowledge my mother for this awareness. In Bali, babies are not removed from the parents presence for six months. They are not allowed even to touch the ground for six months, at which time they are given a spiritual "grounding ceremony." This constant contact with the parents' bodies results in exceptionally good children who grow up to be superior adults. In the six months I was living in Bali, I saw no fear, anger or conflict in the culture.

When it is appropriate, it is a good idea to begin gentle massage on the baby as suggested in Dr. Leboyer's book *Loving Hands*. This is very important and beneficial. During the massage it is good to say affirmations in the second person to the baby.

My good friend Ida Rolf developed the technique for rolfing babies, and several Rolfers are trained to do this. I have discussed this several times with Joe Heller, of the Heller Method, who agrees that if a baby could be aligned immediately after birth, and if the physical effects of the Birth Trauma were removed by this, it would be a miracle. Any damage to the muscular/skeletal system coming out the birth canal could be corrected immediately. It is quite possible that the baby could walk earlier because of this. Leonard once found an article about certain tribes in Africa whose babies were able to walk eight hours after birth because the parents had the thought that this was possible! Look how soon baby animals walk! Are we more evolved, or not?

I, myself, have several times remembered in Rebirthing sessions the intense desire that I had as a baby to walk a lot sooner than I did. *I knew that I could*, but there was so much "mass agreement" on the outside that I couldn't, that I gave up and waited until they thought I could. Think about it. We can offer a lot of theories: e.g., a baby is not coordinated until, _____ and should not walk until, _____ because of _____. But how do we know? Research? Research is based on someone's hypothesis. To prove it, a so-called random sample is "taken." But is it random? If the researcher is trying to prove he is right, he will telepathically attract people who agree with him. What if we left this up to Infinite Intelligence and the spiritual development of the soul? Would infants be walking sooner? How do we know unless we create space for this to happen?

Perhaps we should stay open to the soul who is coming through in the body of a baby and use what *it* wants.

Bonding

Bonding is a nonverbal rapport between parent and child, entailing a relationship process that spiritually ties an infant to the universe of the parents, enabling the child to feel at one with them. This definition, which I like very much, came from Nanci Brown, educator, consultant, writer on birth, bonding and childhood-parenting in the New Age. She goes on to say, in the *Spiritual Community Guide*, the seeds of bonding are planted before birth. The unborn child knows and reacts to the mother's state of mind. Prolonged periods of maternal stresss may result in hyperactivity or fretfulness after birth. (For recent scientific research in this area, please study *The Secret Life of the Unborn Child* by Thomas Verny.)

She recommends that pregnant mothers regularly meditate, practice prenatal yoga or do other centering disciplines (chanting, for example) to help nurture a harmonious bond. *I·· utero* the infant can smile, suck, move, see and respond to sound—and learn. Slow-speed photography has shown that infants as young as eight hours can move their limbs in synchronous response to their mother's voice. Each child has a highly personal response to her mother's words, and indicates a learned pattern begun much earlier in the womb.

Leboyer suggests that mothers who are expecting do a daily hum, repeating it frequently after the birth to re-affirm the bond. A simple spiritual chant or song would serve as well.

Brown emphasizes how important it is to consider carefully the total environment surrounding birth. She says that it is imperative that the child not be separated from the mother at birth. In order to provide the same quality of existence for the infant after birth that it had in the womb, she suggests parents involve themselves in four key elements of the bonding process.

1. Frequent and meaningful eye-to-eye contact
2. Smiling
3. Soothing sounds and words
4. Touch, including carrying and close body contact

This may seem obvious; however, how about having it *very conscious?*

Enlightened Breastfeeding

The main thing about breastfeeding is that the mother be totally relaxed and enjoying herself. Breastfeeding is normal. That it is a pleasurable and sensual experience is normal. It is obviously perfectly natural for the baby. I have rebirthed many people who were not breastfed, and this was a source of great disappointment and anger for them. Often they also had a syndrome of "not enough—what is called the under-nourishment syndrome":

"There is not enough milk for me," and later
"There is not enough love for me," or, as an adult
"There is not enough money for me."

Since WHAT YOU BELIEVE TO BE TRUE YOU CREATE, as we teach in metaphysics, this infant may create a world in which he does not get enough love, nourishment, and money. As far as he is concerned, this is "the way life is." This can happen when someone is "stuck" at the level of breastfeeding. It is something to think about and release.

It is important for the mother to have a good body image and to feel okay about her own breasts. Their size is not important. The milk will come, no matter what, if the mother lets go. The milk will come down if the mother is happy and relaxed. It is important to give up all resentment (towards anyone); resentment blocks the flow. Also, the baby is likely to develop colic because of the heavy negative vibration that resentment brings to a situation. Eating from then on could be uncomfortable and anxiety-producing. A child's table habits and food manners begin long before it can sit at the table. It is obvious, therefore, that the mother should maintain positive thinking during the breastfeeding period. Chanting, singing and listening to music during this time would be very good.

If the mother feels okay about sexual pleasure and about feeling it when her baby sucks on her breasts, she can have a wonderful time and so will the baby, who will learn healthy attitudes about sensuality and sexuality and not pick up guilt. Sexual attitudes begin immediately. The child takes its cue from the parents. What are you putting out on this subject?

The mother should always allow the experience to be as pleasurable for her as possible, and be careful not to "withdraw energy" because of guilt or distractions. Sudden withdrawals of energy or sudden changes of energy are felt as shocking to a baby and you should take extra care in this matter. The baby is responding to *energy* every second, and enough cannot be said on the fact that one handling a baby should always be aware of this. When a parent pulls away abruptly, a child could interpret this as rejection.

In nursing school we even discussed the importance of acknowledging the father's potential jealousy when his wife is breastfeeding the baby. It was suggested that the other breast be offered to him at the same time! This is one way to avoid feeling left out! This lecture obviously stood out in my mind. I cannot report on the effects or any research, but I mention it so that at least this issue is acknowledged. It needs to be discussed.

Touching the Baby
and
Speaking to the Baby

During its infancy there should be frequent handling of the baby in a loving, gentle manner. Love is communicated through touching and stroking, and this is extremely nourishing and healing—especially if parents have worked out their own fear of touching and being touched. This is easily accomplished if you are willing to have it happen. Touching the baby is a magical experience when the parent is focusing on love and saying sweet things to the baby. It is recommended that you speak only in affirmations and certainty, whether you are communicating verbally or nonverbally. I recommend long strokes without jerkily removing the hands. The hands should stay on the body and become warmer and warmer. Please read *Loving Hands: The Traditional Indian Art of Baby Massaging,* by Frederick Leboyer (New York: Knopf, 1976). Try thoughts like these:

"You are wonderful."

"I am so glad that you are here."

"I am always here for you. Even when not physically near, I am still with you in spirit."

"I will take care of you. Everything you need is also inside of you, so you can also take care of yourself."

"You can communicate your needs to me."

"You are very welcome here in our lives."

"We love you completely and unconditionally."

"We accept you completely and unconditionally."

"People love you."

"People are safe."

"You are safe."

"God is always with you."

"God is the Strength in which you can trust."

"There is plenty of everything for you."

"I will listen to you and trust you."

"The Source of Love is inside you."

Speaking in affirmation to your child should be continued throughout infancy and childhood. Children can be enlightened early if they are encouraged in the truth that THOUGHTS CREATE RESULTS and that they can grow up as they please depending on the thoughts they choose. If this is established immediately, even though the schools may not recognize it, the foundation for the child will be built, and it can create its own perfect universe, making parenting easy.

Lying in Bed with the Newborn

I think you can see the incredible advantage of allowing the baby to be in bed with *both* of its parents *all day for several days* after the birth. The parents can easily arrange for someone they love and trust to serve the three in bed. Massage is also in order for the trio. Taking time for these things will be more than worth it in later life. This cannot be stressed enough.

Writing in *The Continuum Concept* (New York: Alfred A. Knopf, Inc.), Jean Liedloff notes:

The period immediately following the birth is the most impressive part of life outside of the mother's body. Every nerve ending under his newly exposed skin craves the expected embrace, all his being the character of all he is, leads to his being held in arms.

The state of consciousness of an infant changes enormously during the in-arms phase. He is building a framework that will become his for life. If he feels safe, wanted, and "at home," his view of later experiences will be very distinct in character from those of a child who feels unwelcome and unstimulated (pp.54-56).

Baby Massage

Massage is a high expression of love that continues the bonding process, establishing a warm, positive parent-child relationship. I suggest you read the book *Baby Massage* by Australian author Amelia Auckett and *Loving Hands* by Dr. Frederick Leboyer.

Holding the Newborn

There can never be too much holding of a newborn. Body contact and touch is the most important thing of all. The parent's touch should be one of love, gentleness and, at the same time, certainty. If the parent has fear of holding the baby because it is "too fragile," the baby could grow up with limiting programming and be afraid of life.

Jean Liedloff, author of the excellent book *The Continuum Concept*, (New York: Alfred Knopf, Inc.), addresses these points thoroughly; she bases her beliefs on careful studies of primitive South American Indians. These Indians grew up to be very secure within themselves, and Ludloff concluded that their security was directly related to the way they were continually held as infants. She points out that the period immediately following birth is the most impressive part of life outside the mother's body. This is the first impression of life! The leap from the hospitality of the womb should be made to the parents' arms.

Under the continuum concept, infants are taken everywhere. During the "in-arms phase," the baby experiences being next to the mother's body all the time. This practice, as I mentioned earlier, is used in Bali, and I saw the wonderful effects myself. The baby learns much more by having so many safe experiences and it also learns to balance its head on its body. The baby learns many more postures than it would lying in a crib untouched.

The author suggests literally keeping the baby's body next to the mother's at all times until the baby naturally choses more independence, which it will when it is ready. This takes away any negative feelings of abandonment or separation, and the torment of longing to be held.

The more activity the mother has while the baby is next to her body, the better. She says a mother sitting still all the time will condition the baby to think life is dull. Also (and this is important), if the mother treats the baby as fragile, it will be.

In that culture, and others Ludloff studies, babies nurse much more often than in our culture. She showed how this is much more beneficial than our way, which is often limited by scheduling, inconvenience and embarrassment.

In regard to bonding, which she calls *imprinting*, the author discusses what a momentous event occurs as soon as the birth is complete: The mother and child are meeting as separate individuals for the first time.

What happens if this imprinting is not allowed to occur? What happens if the baby is taken away when the mother is keyed to caress it, to bring it to her breast, into her arms and into her heart; or if the mother is too drugged to experience the bonding fully; what happens? It appears that the stimulous to imprint, if not responded to by the expected meeting with the baby, gives way to a state of grief.

I recall rebirthing many people who sobbed for hours over the separation and lack of bonding.

In the maternity wards of Western civilization there is little chance of consolation . . . . The newborn infant, with his skin crying out for the ancient touch of smooth, warmth radiating, living flesh, is wrapped in dry, lifeless cloth. He is put in a box where he is left, no matter how he weeps, in a limbo that is utterly motionless. The only sounds he can hear are the wails of other victims of the same ineffable agony. The sound can mean nothing to him. He cries and cries; his lungs, new to air, are strained with the desperation in his heart. No one comes. Trusting in the rightness of life, as by nature he must, he does the only act he can, which is to cry on. Eventually, a timeless lifetime later, he falls asleep exhausted.

What a Tragedy!

PAY ATTENTION! Learn from the primitive Indian tribes and the animals who are happy and healthy following instincts and Infinite Intelligence.

I want to stress the importance of the father's holding the baby. I have rebirthed many women who were held quite a lot by their mothers when they were infants, but hardly at all by their fathers. These women had grown up feeling "untouched" by a man and with many unconscious decisions about that, which later produced the result in their relationships that the man they loved the most would not touch them. They then became bitter and resentful towards their mates, and this resulted in even less touching. Many would leave their mates in search of touching they longed for, only to recreate the situation again and again with other partners.

Rocking

I personally feel that every household with a newborn should have a rocker. One must remember that the baby, while *in utero*, was rocked continually during the nine months by the physical movements of the mother, and also by the movement of the diaphragm as the mother breathed. A baby just out of the uterus, therefore, loves to be rocked because it is familiar and feels secure. It is also soothing to the mother, and an enjoyable way to breastfeed.

Diaper Changing

I have rebirthed many people who were able to distinctly re-member the feelings that went on during diaper changing. For example, many men were able to remember that when their mother got to the genital area, she withdrew her energy in embarrassment, and often the baby boy made a decision. "There must be something wrong with that part of my body." (It could be that this psychic shock prevented him from growing his penis to the size it might have been. Think about it.) This diaper-changing time, plus the psychic and physical trauma of circumcision, must be explored further.

An infant rapidly becomes aware of its mother's reaction when the diaper needs changing. Does the mother make re-jecting sounds? Does she turn her head in disgust? Does she indicate she does not like cleaning the baby and making him comfortable? Are her eyes cold and does she want to hurry and get it over with? Are the movements rough? The baby is extremely sensitive to all this, and chances are it will be flooded with fear and guilt. Psycho-sexual development can be blocked if the person changing diapers cannot handle the intimacy of that moment. Of course, the same applies to the father, or to anyone else who changes the baby.

Part II

Report on the First International Congress on Pre- and Peri-natal Psychology

(July 8-10, 1983   Toronto, Ontario, Canada
organized by Dr. Thomas Verny, author of
The Secret Life of the Unborn Child)

This congress represented the collective enthusiasm of professionals in many disciplines who are exploring the mental and emotional development of the unborn and the very young child. These people are all extremely interested in improving the well-being of future generations. Some of the sessions, conducted by professionals from all over the world, were research-orientated, some were practical how-to sessions, and others were meant to be thought-provoking.

Ernest Freud talked about the fact that the baby is generally cared for by a male obstetrician and pediatrician, and related this to the fact that men have exclusion anxiety. He talked about placental changes due to heavy smoking of the pregnant mother—and even of the father.

Dr. Michael Odent, who has now done 100 underwater births in France, seemed to me to be the "star" of the congress. His films of underwater birth were amazing. He began his presentation by making the following statement: "We need to create a new being who has a maximum capacity to love."

Sheila Kitzinger, childbirth educator, social anthropologist, and author of a dozen books, closed the congress with a dynamic speech encouraging women to "reclaim their bodies" during childbirth and not give away their power to the male-dominated medical profession. She talked about labor and delivery in the Third World. In some cultures she visited, women experienced an ecstatic worship—laboring in *spirit*—and shouted passages from the Bible during contractions. They were allowed to *be who they were* completely; no male system was imposed upon them. Sheila received a standing ovation. (Her books are listed in the bibliography.)

I was honored to speak at this congress, representing rebirthing in the world. I acknowledge my friend, Dr. Tom Verny, who masterminded the first congress, and I acknowledge all the great presenters who have committed themselves to this work.

For more information on the past and future congresses (held every two years in odd-numbered years), please contact:

    PPPANA
    Pre- and Peri-natal Psychology Association
      of North America
    36 Madison Avenue
    Toronto, Ontario M5R   2F1
    CANADA

Dr. Odent's Birth Reborn

Michel Odent is a leading figure in the worldwide movement to reform and humanize birth, which in this country inspires efforts to open birth centers, introduce birthing chairs, revitalize midwifery, admit husbands to delivery rooms, and generally make the hospital atmosphere more sensitive to the needs of mothers and newborns. Dr. Odent has been the subject of numerous articles in popular and medical journals throughout the world, of documentaries for German and Japanese television, and of a BBC film *Birth Reborn* which has been credited with bringing about "extraordinary changes in British hospitals" (Sheila Kitzinger). Dr. Odent is the "hottest property in obstetrics today" (Doris Haire), and his presence on a program guarantees heated controversy and standing ovations. Twelve hundred people came to hear him at a recent San Francisco Conference on Technology and Obstetrics sponsored by *Birth* magazine. He has lectured at Harvard, Yale, and other major medical schools in this country. American professionals—physicians, midwives, nurses—have either heard him or heard about him. They will want to read his first available presentation of his ideas and practices.

Most women in this country still give birth in hospitals, reluctant to trust non-medical alternatives like home births or lay midwives (99% in 1980; 96% in 1983—a change which reflects the increased use of birth centers). *Birth Reborn* speaks to them. It is the first book *by a doctor* practicing *in a hospital* which offers practical strategies and solutions for their dissatisfactions.

In a state hospital in a small town in Northern France, Dr. Michel Odent, a French physician frequently compared with Dr. Leboyer for his influence on childbirth practices, has created a revolution in modern obstetrics. *Without screening of any kind*, cesarian rates, episiotomy rates, and postpartum depression figures in the world. As worldwide alarm over the state of obstetrics rises, the remarkably impressive results at Pithiviers—where birth is *active, truly natural,* and part of the *affective, intimate life* of the woman and couple—provide dramatic evidence that Dr. Odent's approach offers safety for mother and child even as it transforms the experience of childbirth. Evidence, too, of just how much can be done in a hospital setting to humanize and dignify childbirth.

Now, for the first time, Dr. Odent presents his revolutionary methods to an American audience. Mixing personal reflections and medical information, unusually striking photographs and moving stories by women who gave birth at his clinic, Dr. Odent offers a clear, detailed, practical depiction of what birth at Pithiviers is like. We follow the events from the moment a woman arrives, through the birth of her first contacts with the child, until the moment she leaves for home. Odent's methods are simple:

- Women are free to walk around during labor and to give birth any way they choose—standing, sitting, squatting, even resting in water. They are never compelled to lie on their backs in the traditional "stranded beetle" position—the single most difficult, inefficient, and painful position for the woman, and the most dangerous for the baby.
- Birth is never induced; Odent never uses drugs, painkillers, or forceps, and resorts to technological and surgical intervention only in emergencies.
- Mother and infant remain together in the hours after birth to facilitate bonding.
- Midwives and partners play a central role in creating a warm and reassuring environment.

Odent's tone is always commonsensical, charming, and mild. Yet, like Leboyer in his time, Odent now challenges the central beliefs of conventional obstetrics: that pregnancy is a special kind of illness, that routine technological intervention is necessary to ensure safety, that women, for their own good, should lie back and leave it to the doctors. His book, like his clinic, offers a model, sure to be adopted, of how birth can be reborn as a normal, natural, and confident part of life.

Rebirthing Before and During Pregnancy

The supremely ideal birth to me would be where both parents had released their own birth trauma *before conception* of a child. This is my idea of perfection because there would be little or no psychic contamination to the fetus and little fear of the birth itself.

This could be done easily and pleasurably if both parents were willing to get rebirthed for at least a year prior to conceiving a child. The guidance of a spiritual master who is powerful enough to wash out birth trauma is also extremely helpful. It is interesting to speculate that the clearer they are of these factors, the more enlightened a soul the parents could attract to bring in.

As rebirthers, we have seen that mothers who have been rebirthed a lot during pregnancy have an easier delivery. They tend to report that their babies "came out like butter." It was of course extremely helpful that the mother could do the rebirthing breath during labor and delivery.

Divine Childbirth
and Rebirthing

by Rima Beth Star

(RIMA BETH STAR, M.A., is a counselor in private practice in Austin, Texas. She is a nationally respected rebirther, seminar leader, and co-leader of the "Loving Me, Loving You, Loving All" Relationship Training. She and her husband, Steven Star, coordinate Theta Texas Seminars and are members of the Lutheran Church.)

I met some midwives at a Healing Arts Festival and began, soon after our meeting, to rebirth several of them. One day they called me and asked me to assist them at a birth. The pregnant woman, Susan, was a midwife herself from another city. This was her second child, her first being born in a hospital. Her waters had broken two days earlier and she had not gone into labor. The other midwives in her city were scared and wanted her to go to a hospital. Instead, they agreed to call the Austin midwives, who I assumed had more experience, and brought her to them for "one last try."

When I arrived at the home, there were about twelve adults there and several children. Many of them were very agitated and in a "tizzie" over the fact that Susan was not yet in labor. When I walked into her room, I saw a very "up-tight" woman being threatened with going to the hospital if she didn't go into labor by morning, and I also saw love and concern from these people and a desire to do what was best.

Susan and I were left alone and began talking. I shared with her about affirmations, thoughts, breathing. The first affirmation I gave her was, "It is safe for me to have my perfect healthy baby, at the perfect time, here at home or in the hospital, either place is perfectly safe." She started crying immediately and fears of hospitals and doctors came gushing to the surface. She said she was so afraid of having to go to the hospital, that she couldn't let herself have her baby now. At this time her husband arrived and was very loving and supportive. I left them together for a while.

When I returned, Susan looked like a different person. We talked about her past conclusions and how they no longer needed to affect her reality now. She could indeed have a safe birth wherever she was, and she knew that this was true.

I suggested that she relax and do some gentle breathing and just "be" with herself and her baby. She breathed through two cycles of energy, seeing scenes from her own birth, an appendix operation, childhood memories, love and laughter from parents and friends, and all the while feeling safe and at peace. She was radiant and happy. We talked loving affirmations to her baby and had a wonderful time. At the end of her second cycle, she began having contractions and really was present for the rhythm and movement of labor. The midwives assisting her were very competent and loving. Five hours later out popped a radiant, breathing, divine girl.

I concluded that trusting divinity, rebirthing and thinking positively works! Rebirthing does assist people in releasing and clearing birth trauma, and I expanded my commitment to work with parents, pregnant women, and birth personnel. I believe that people who choose to have a child should be able to relax for the child's birth, free from fears and a feeling of emergency.

Being present at this birth was a fantastic opportunity for me. I had a son in 1968 who drowned four years later. During this birth, my memory bank on the subject of birth was flung wide open and I was able to release on thoughts that I hadn't looked at in years. What I chose to do was to let go of every thought that came to my consciousness that *expected* labor and birth to be difficult, hard, traumatic, or emergency-oriented. I allowed myself to see the truth of birthing for me then, without the blinders of limiting thoughts that I had previously. *What I saw was a wholly divine experience of love, flow and pleasure, complete with radiant light flowing within us, around us, above us, through us. I saw birth as the ordinary, miraculous experience that it is.* I realized births are always this way, even when our egos and limiting belief systems try to separate us from the divine order of which we are a part.

So, let's accept the simplicity, ease, safety and normalcy of birthing a divine child into the world. Let's witness to our trust that the universe is a safe and appropriate place for the ordinary miracle of birth. Let's allow any thoughts which do not support what we know is true to simply disappear like the nothingness which they *truly* are. Let's follow the infallible guidance we receive from our Higher Self, trusting that when we choose in harmony with our Divine Spirit, or Higher Self, we are choosing what is best for all concerned.

After this experience, I began doing clearing processes with rebirthers on their/our present-time beliefs about births. What I discovered is a lot of willingness to move through resistances to looking at birth as a present-time phenomena, instead of only as "that past traumatic event that I can now release on through rebirthing."

Some of the processes I use are—"A fear I have about having/ not having children is _____. Something I like about having/not having children is _____. Conscious childbirth to me means _____."

One of the things *conscious* childbirth means to me now is coming from a place of freedom and choice so that having, or not having, a child is totally unrelated to parental, societal, or other conditioned belief systems—so that we're not trying to please our parents, or complete our woman- or manhood, or be immortal through our kids, leaving a little part of ourselves behind when we are dead and gone, or creating someone who will give us the unconditional love that we won't give ourselves, or thinking that not having kids means we are more spiritually enlightened, or thinking that having kids means we are more spiritual enlightened. When we can truly say, "I AM TOTALLY A DIVINE, PERFECT, OK, FULFILLED BEING WHETHER I DO OR DO NOT HAVE A CHILD. MY SELF-ESTEEM, WELL-BEING AND APPROVAL IS NOT DEPENDENT ON MY HAVING

OR NOT HAVING A CHILD," we can then be pretty sure that we're into a freer and clear space.

The decision to have or not have children can then arise from a place of pristine purity where pure white light and love is the only substance from which we create, or do not create, form (babies).

Mother Mary was conscious that the divine life within her was the Christ child. She had certainty! An angel appeared to her saying, "Hail O favored one, the Lord is with you . . . the child to be born will be called holy." And Mary replied, "Behold, I am the handmaid of the Lord; let it be to me according to your word." (Luke I:26-35). We too are like Mary. We can say, "Let it be to me according to God's word," or "Let it be to me according to my Higher Self." We do not have to worry whether "having" or "not having" a child is right or wrong for us. We can be willing to see the truth of our constant connection with Infinite Intelligence which knows the Divine Plan of our lives. Let's remove our trust in Ego and lower-self tricksters and *BE* in the natural flow of our own divinity.

Mary had so much trust in the Word of God that physical sexual union was not even an intermediary step. Mary did not have physical sexual union with Joseph and she birthed a son, Christ Jesus. The common belief that physical bodies are created through physical sexual union was proved to be just that, a belief system, and nothing more. It is certainly fine, appropriate, and divine to create children through thought and physical sexual union, AND it is good to remember that it is not mandatory. We, like Mary, have that spark of Christ light within us. We can choose to magnify our Godliness and become more and more free of the world of separation and unforgiveness.

It is also not mandatory to use contraceptive devices, other than the "contra" ception of consciously choosing thoughts which oppose, or are contrary to, having a child. The best *contra, con*-ception I know of is to release negative, limiting thoughts about pregnancy and childbirth, to come from choice and trust in the purity of our connection with

Divine Intelligence. What I frequently tell people is, "If you have any doubts about stopping use of popular contraceptives, then don't stop. If you have total certainty that YOU are in harmony with the Source of all creation, then it doesn't matter whether you use contraceptives or not." If you choose to have a child you can do so under any conditions. You don't have to "work" at trying or not trying to get pregnant.

Birth has very little to do with sex, or contraception, and a lot to do with Thought, Contemplation, Visualization and Communion. As stated in *The Life and Teachings of the Masters of the Far East:*

> *Pure white light is God life . . . As we fix and focalize our ideal through contemplation, the vision takes life, stands forth, comes closer and closer, until our vision and the form are united and stand forth as ourselves, and become one with us; then we become that. Thus we say to all mankind "I AM YOURSELF EXPRESSING GOD." When the true mother sees this at the time of conception, the immaculate conception takes place; then there is no rebirth. This is womanhood, manhood, wo-man-hood is God—the true Godhead of all humanity. (p.118)*

As used above, "Wo" represents Yin, or the Feminine Principle, and "Man" represents Yang, or Masculine Principle. "Wo" also represents Energy or Light, and "Man" represents Thought or Word. "Hood" represents Union or Connection. The Union of Energy, "Wo", and Thought, "Man," creates Physical Form. All physical form is created by the union of Energy and Thought, "Wo" and "Man," whether that form is a baby, an event, or a typewriter. All of us have "Wo" and "Man", Energy and Thought, as actualities within ourselves. We are complete and whole within ourselves. Achieving "womanhood" or "manhood" means we have accepted the source of creation, the union of Energy and Thought within ourselves.

Creation of a child has, in truth, nothing to do with the sex of our body, or our partner's body, and a whole lot to do with focusing and connecting Energy and Thought. It is possible to materialize a body directly out of pure consciousness, and it is OK if we choose a more conventional birth process, like nine months. My point is: We all have male and female energies within ourselves. We are not only male or female, but ONE BEING, complete, whole and divine. We are capable of creating form through the union of the masculine and femine principles of God within ourselves. We can remember the Source of our creation and choose to be in Harmony with that Source.

I have been doing more and more teaching on childbirth and rebirthing, and being open to the highest quality thoughts on birth that I know of. The Austin Lay Midwives are now integrating techniques, like rebirthing, which lead to more and more conscious childbirth into their education program, and find their clients loving this approach. I have found the rebirthing breathing process, the affirmations technique, and commitment to a spiritual family of your choice, combine to create safe and loving births for all concerned. The breathing process assists in clearing the body/mind of stored trauma and tension. The affirmation process assists in clearing the subconscious of limiting, non-supporting thoughts and commitment to a spiritual family provides us reinforcement for a life in service to God.

Here are some of the affirmations we have created. It is helpful to write them, say them, listen to them on tape, until you feel they are a natural, flowing part of your consciousness:

1. I am responsible for being, or not being, pregnant.
2. Pregnancy is natural, normal, healthy, vibrant, safe and divine for me and my baby.
3. I, (name), offer my perfect, healthy, divine body to be used to nurture and present a Christ child to the world.

4. My child is not conceived in sin and born into iniquity, but is pure, sacred and holy, conceived of God and Goddess, born of God, the image or Christ of God.

5. Christ is in me, in my partner, and in my baby.

6. I now allow the Christ Light to stand forth from within me and my baby.

7. Seeing my baby is seeing the Christ of God face to face.

8. The universe loves and supports me and my baby.

9. I can communicate with the spirit of my child before and during pregnancy, and always.

10. It is safe for me to have my perfect, healthy baby, at the perfect time, in the perfect way, with the perfect people.

11. Birthing is a time of pleasure. There is nothing to be feared.

12. Breathing and trust combine to create a joyful, transcendental birthing experience.

13. Contractions (rushes) are my friend and each rhythm and movement brings me closer to the birth of my baby.

14. I am calm and relaxed. My baby feels my calmness and shares it.

15. The baby and I are ready for the Divine Plan of our lives to unfold.

16. The baby is naturally doing just what she or he should.

17. The movements of my uterus are massaging and hugging my baby.

18. The baby is descending naturally. The baby's head fits perfectly in my pelvis.

19. My vagina expands easily as the baby's head crowns, then emerges. I see God and Goodness, and Myself.

Rebirthing Explained

Leonard Orr, founder of rebirthing:

As new yoga, rebirthing is not a discipline. It is an inspiration. It is not teaching a person how to breathe, it is the intuitive gentle act of learning how to breathe from the breath itself. It is connecting the inhale with the exhale in a relaxed, intuitive rhythm until the inner breath, which is the Spirit and source of breath itself, is merged with air—the outer breath.

The purpose of rebirthing is to remember and re-experience birth. The experience begins a transformation of the subconscious impression of birth from one of primal pain to one of pleasure. Effects on life are immediate: as negative energy patterns held in the mind and body start to dissolve, "youthing" replaces aging, and life becomes more fun.

Denise Gilman, rebirther:

Rebirthing is a safe and gentle breathing process that releases accumulated negativity back to and including birth. Through this process, unwanted behavior patterns are revealed and released, and the heart opens so you can receive more love, peace, and abundance. Rebirthing is a powerful healing tool on mental, emotional, physical and spiritual levels. A Rebirth Training is a wonderful way of being introduced to rebirthing, continuing your rebirth process, or applying the training toward becoming a professional rebirther.

To find a rebirther, call (212) 799-7324.

Meditation for Childbirth

by Tara Ibbie White

OM TARA TUTTH TARA
TURE MAMA AI YUG
PUNYEH BYANA PUNTING
GURU SOHA
—Mantra for the White Tara

Breath moving easily in and out
a poem of Light filling
the receptacle of your heart.

Deep abdominal breath
refining each breath
a movement of expansion
on the in-breath
and a movement of acceptance
on the out-breath

Visualizing within your body
the emergent infant
        body
            and
speak to the
soul force:

"If it is your time
to enter
this Plane of Being
Push, Little Baby, now."

Relax
expand the cervix
as the child bears down
and on the in-breath
focus your attention
upward
moving from the uterus,
lungs, third eye, crown chakra
focusing at a point
above the top of your head
mingling your soul essence
with the essence of the
incoming child.

And on the exhalation
pull in—ever so gently—
not too fast—
the angelic Light Force
that surrounds you
on either side
extending in radiant astral colors
wings from your shoulders

Bring the breath in
through the top of your head
to your heart
to your uterus
penetrating with the breath
the peak moment of contraction
extending the sensation
        of pain
beyond its limiting barriers
carrying you and the child
in the pleasure of ecstacy
beyond Light

In labor
breathe deeply
oxygenate the uterus
don't think
just be
you'll never be in this place again
relax the hips, thighs, knees, calves,
shins, ankles, toes and feet

Jai Ma!

Tara Ibbe White is a San Francisco Bay Area writer, astrologer, palmist and mother, who leads women's groups in meditation and natural birthing.

Part III

The Miracle of Underwater Birth

When I first heard about underwater birth in Russia, I thought it was a miracle. As a rebirther, it made total sense to me! It seemed to be such a great breakthrough in reducing and preventing the birth trauma. In nursing, I had realized that *prevention* of disease was the answer, rather than trying to do something when it was often too late. In rebirthing I soon saw that although we could do something about correcting the effects of the birth trauma, it made more sense to prevent it in the first place. I had become very interested in Dr. Leboyer's work in France (i.e., the "quiet birth," where the baby was put in water right after birth to soothe it, relax it). I had the privilege of meeting Dr. Leboyer and being a part of his first tour to the U.S. But when I heard of underwater birth, I was more than excited. I could see unlimited possibilities, and intuitively I knew how this method would enhance the life of the new being. There was no question in my mind that it would be fantastic.

I was delighted to see my colleagues (rebirthers) who were pregnant go for it. They understood it right away. I was honored that rebirthers in our community were the first in the U.S. to try this method, and that I was chosen to be the godmother of one of these underwater babies a year-and-a-half later. I was privileged to go to France and meet Dr. Michael Odent, who has now done 100 underwater births at the General Hospital of Pithiviers, 50 miles south of Paris. Seeing the setup there and hearing him talk about it made me even more enthusiastic about underwater birth (sometimes called the "Russian Method").

I became very passionate about the whole thing. We had film footage that was very exciting from Mela Noel's birth, and from the birth of Jeremy, the first underwater baby in the U.S., who was born to Patrick and Jia Lighthouse. I wanted to share this with the world. I even went on Grass

Roots TV in Aspen, Colorado during the summer Rebirther's Jubilee. Underwater birth was suddenly a very hot item. But then it became difficult to deal with in the media— not just because it was controversial and new. There was a race to get these films into Hollywood. I did not like the greed reactions of the filmmakers who wanted to get involved. I felt the sacredness of it all was being abused, so I started to back off and withdraw my energy.

I "shelved" whatever grandiose projects had been dreamed up and went into a cooling-off period. I hibernated and did not talk about it much. And yet there was Mela, my god-daughter, the result of an underwater birth. She impressed me as an outstanding being. She would actually "appear" to me throughout that year in my dreams, and even in waking hours during rebirths and my meditations. Sometimes I would see her "upside down" laughing, as if she were coming out of the womb and enjoying it. She was not even two years old during this period.

Igor Charkowsky started the Russian underwater birth technique. The mother sits inside a glass tank during the last stages of labor. The water level is at her shoulders. When the infant emerges, he or she floats in the water and continues to breathe through the umbilical cord for about 10 minutes. Then the child is removed from the water and the umbilical cord is cut. The effect of the water is to reduce stress for both mother and child. Charkovsky has a great belief in the thera-peutic value of water. Being in the water calms the mother and brings the baby into the world in a placid state. The baby comes from a liquid environment into a liquid environ-ment. The light is less intense. It is a *gradual* introduction into the world.

Charkowsky was influenced by the philosophy of Kon-stantin Tsiolkovsky, a pioneer Russian space scientist who believed that humans are destined to live in space or on other planets, where their bodies would develop differently than on earth. In places where there is less gravitational pull, human beings would need less energy to move around, he theorized. There would be more energy available to the brain. The supposition is that babies born in other gravitational fields could have large brain cavities. By learning to accommodate in more than one gravitational field, one builds up adaptability in the brain. Immersion in water can simulate some of the feelings of weightlessness found in space. This is the foundation of Charkowsky's insistence on daily swimming for all young babies. He takes babies as young as 13 days old and has them swimming 45 minutes every day.

Most medical men agree, that as a baby leaves the womb it feels an immense heaviness—a powerful gravitational shock. This is why the baby's oxygen consumption jumps three- to four-fold. All the infant's energy goes into neutralizing the gravitational force. The water birth reduces the trauma of the introduction to gravity.

Dr. Charkovsky, in an article called "Adaptation to Water Environment: Perspectives Towards Progressive Evolution of Man," states the following:

> Twenty years ago my first daughter was born prematurely. She weighed only 1.2 kilos and doctors said she was hopeless. I placed her into a water environment, thus in fact returning her to the world where she was safe. It wouldn't be an overstatement to say that she spent in water the first two years of her life. Very soon we had no more fears regarding her condition. She became far more advanced both physically and intellectually than most of the children her age.
>
> Actually that was the first experiment to prove the assumption that artifically prolonged state of suspension creates better conditions for maturation and development of the brain tissue. The brain of a baby weighs one-seventh of its body. For an adult it is only 2 percent. This suggests that under the conditions of gravity more energy is required to live and the priority is given to the development of such elements as lungs, stomach, organs of digestion and secretion, etc. A larger brain re-

quires a more powerful energy supply system. During the first moments of life the most sensitive nerve cells collapse under the conditions of high content of oxygen as strong irritants. The conditions of gravity ensure that only the toughest, the crudest, elements of the organism survive, while the most valuable and delicate ones collapse during the first minutes and hours of life.

It has been proved experimentally that new babies are capable of holding their breath for a considerably longer time than adults. The baby delivered underwater will avoid the ill-effects of the gravitational environment and preserve many of the brain cells which otherwise would be inevitably destroyed. There is no danger that the baby will immediately choke with water and die of asphyxia. But the weak point of the new baby is that his biological field is open and extremely responsive to many different kinds of suggestions. The fear that the majority of people experience when they see their child in the water making what seems to be helpless movements seems to be the most dangerous factor. We used to use the assistance of people in Russia we called "sensitives," possessing . . . extrasensory capacities. But they are too rare to use their assistance on a regular basis. The problem is to work out methods of overcoming fear.

Regarding underwater deliveries, I would like to comment here that what we have been doing in the U.S. to overcome this fear is to have the parents rebirthed properly before delivery so that this fear is already alieviated. We also have other Rebirthers present at the birth to help alieviate any unexpected fear. Ideally, a couple has done wet rebirthing and therefore the water is familiar and safe to all involved. This will be elaborated upon later in this chapter. I would like to see water training exercises become popular for babies (Read the book *Water Babies*, by Erik Sindebladh [New York: St. Martin's Press, 1983].).

Dr. Charkowsky states that one of the necessary conditions for overcoming this fear is publicity. Questions of underwater deliveries and water exercises for new babies should be discussed on all levels. He feels that another effective tool is to facilitate contacts with mothers who have already performed underwater deliveries. This is obvious, and in the U.S. we do make a strong attempt to get these people together with those who want to do it. Charkovsky also recommends swimming exercises for future mothers themselves. He further states:

> Finally a few words regarding the threat of infection. In the majority of experiments I used ordinary unprocessed water and there have been no cases of infection.
>
> A couple of years ago we experimented with underwater deliveries in the Black Sea and our assistants were dolphins. Apart from their striking intelligence, dolphins possess a very strong and favorable biological field. There are plenty of data available that in the presence of dolphins people suddenly cease to fear water. Legends circulate of dolphins having rescued people from drowning in the sea. In our experiments, dolphins provided for an excellent psychic environment in which both mothers and babies felt quite at home.

In the *Birth and Family Journal* (Vol. 8), Dr. Michel Odent discusses underwater birth in an article called "The Evolution of Obstetrics at Pithiviers:"

> We have also discovered the efficiency of water in the first stage of labor. The reason why kneeling or immersion in water during labor is so helpful is mysterious. What is clear is that water is often the way to reduce inhibitions. Some enter a different level of consciousness in water, seeming to dream. Others find it easier to relax when immersed in water. And we observe that during such immersion in warm water, semi-darkness is the best way to reach a high level of relaxation. Water

114

may be a good way to reduce adrenergic secretion. Immersion in warm water with semi-darkness may also be a way to reach alpha brainwave rhythms. Water may be a symbol of mother, of comfort, regression to childlike needs and behavior. Whatever way we want to talk about the effect of water during labor, one thing is sure. The contractions become more efficient and less painful at the same time, so that sometimes the labor is very quick. Many women do not want to leave the pool because it is so comfortable. As a result sometimes the baby comes while the mother is in the pool.

Recommended reading, Dr. Odent's *Birth Reborn* (New York: Pantheon).

The Results of Underwater Birth

Apart from reduced trauma, underwater babies do things conventional babies find impossible. Often after two or three months they can stand and at six months they can walk. Dr. Charkovsky's experiments also show that the underwater babies who do the swimming program lack any fear of water, are more confident, lack aggression, and are more intelligent than conventional babies. They rarely fall sick, easily withstand cold and weather changes, do not have temper tantrums, sleep soundly, and are physically stronger, more active, brighter and more resourceful than average.

The Underwater Birth
of Jeremy Lighthouse

On October 28, 1981 in San Diego, California, Jia Lighthouse and her husband Patrick gave birth to the first underwater baby in the U.S. (to my knowledge). The baby stayed under water for about 20 minutes, still receiving oxygen from the placenta, before coming up for his first gentle breaths. Initially motivated by pictures of Russian water births, both Patrick and Jia felt that underwater childbirth would eliminate much of the human birth trauma. In her first delivery of an older son, Jia had 36 hours of terrifying labor and a retained placenta, and both she and that baby almost died. That birth experience came about even after tremendous preparation. Five years later, after a lot of emotional release through rebirthing and affirmations, she enjoyed a labor of only 2½ hours and delivered a 10½ pound baby underwater.

Jia and Patrick prepared for the water birth at the physical level by renting a fiberglass spa and setting up a birth room in their double garage with drapes, carpets, plants, and pictures. After sterilizing the tub, they filled it with distilled water to control bacteria. They also added salt to approximate the density of amniotic fluid and heated the water to 101° F., the womb temperature.

The Lighthouses held several clearing meetings with their birthing crew, three men and three women who were all rebirthers, to make sure no one would bring any fear, whether from their own unconscious birth trauma or from the water aspect of this birth. They were unable to find any medical person willing to be involved. When the contractions became intense quickly, it was with great relief that Jia sank into the tub of water. She experimented with different positions. Within 30 minutes she found herself on hands and knees ready to push. The heat and buoyancy of the water afforded her great assistance. In spite of Jeremy's size, she did not tear a bit. Jeremy was, rightfully, caught by his father, with a midwife in the background for consultation. As in any Leboyer birth, Jia immediately cradled him to her breast, still totally submerged. Patrick monitored both the cord and Jeremy's heartbeat at all times. (During his 20-minute "swim," Jeremy sometimes kicked, sometimes floated with his father's assistance, and sometimes slept, just as in the womb. When Jia passed a large blood clot, they knew the placenta was detaching, and it was time for Jeremy to surface and begin lung breathing. He had another full 20 minutes of placental oxygen in which to learn to breathe on his own.

Jia acknowledges the many benefits in choosing underwater birth: It is comfortable for the baby's body, she says, and lessens the shock and sensory overload so typical for the newborn. She also adds that the freedom of movement within familiar fluid surroundings, yet without boundaries or the experience of gravity, provides a sense of security which allows the baby to draw positive conclusions about this world. The underwater birth reduces the separation trauma felt by both mother and infant at birth by creating a new transition stage: out of the womb, yet physically, and therefore psychologically, still connected via the umbilical cord (which is not "shut down" from exposure to cold air). Jia loved the fact that there was no need to take Jeremy away from her.

Because the environment of the hot tub and the womb are so similar, Jeremy could relax immediately after the stress of the birth canal. This, Jia explains, provides the ideal learning situation described in *The Magical Child* (New York: Bantam, 1980) by Joseph Chilton Pearce. Recent research has shown that we learn more at the moment of birth than at any other time of our lives. However, for this learning to have a positive effect, Pearce says, infants must be able to extend their sense of the familiar into their new surroundings. With the underwater birth, Jeremy simply expanded his experience of the womb. Significantly, he enlarged it enough to include his father, which facilitated their close bond.

I would like to thank Patrick and Jia for this presentation.

The Underwater Birth
of Mela Noel Star

My goddaughter, Mela Noel, was born on November 5, 1981 in Austin, Texas to Rima Beth and Steven Star, after her parents had been inspired by the birth of Jeremy Lighthouse in California. Rima and Steve went to the feed store and purchased a 6 × 3 foot cattle trough (in true Texas spirit!) and painted it white. The tub was filled with three feet of warm tap water and refined salt solution. Rima's cervix was completely dilated when she and Steven got into the tub. About 30 minutes later, Steven was holding his daughter as she slept under the water, the umbilical cord still attached and pulsating. Since she was getting everything that she needed they decided not to rush her. "She seemed at peace," Rima said, "like she was at home."

For almost 7 minutes, Mela dozed in the water as her parents, three midwives and a few friends watched. Then she opened her eyes, stretched her tiny body and smiled at them as if she were saying "Hi." Rima and Steven like to think of their daughter's birth as a perfect birth—the ideal birth!

I was in India at the time of the birth, but I flew to Austin as soon as I could to interview Rima and Steve about this miracle.

Interview with Rima Beth Star, Mela's Mother

Sondra: Rima, how did you ever get involved in the idea of having what you call an ideal birth?

R: Well, for me it started back when I had a child in 1968; I was very young, and I didn't know anything about birth. I thought you went to the hospital and had a shot and came

120

out with a baby. My first delivery was very traumatic and intense, and a lot of times I thought I was dying or something horrible was happening. I was unprepared, and afterwards I just . . . I felt that there had to be a better way. I didn't know about birth trauma. I didn't know about any of those things. I just knew in my heart that there was a better way to be, and to live, and to know about birth. So, as the years went by, I kept searching for ways to make my life happier and to feel better, because . . . I didn't even want to be here if I'm not going to have satisfaction. Why be here? So my main search in life was to figure out how to live life fully and happily, and how other people could have that experience. This led me into being a sociologist and sharing with people in that way. Through studying other cultures I became interested in the individual process of healing, and I began studying different techniques, therapies, psychologies and yogas. At one point I became very much aware of my breath—how it was tight and constricted, and it seemed that I just couldn't breathe well. Then a little sign went off in my head that said: "Rebirthing. Remember rebirthing," which I had heard of a year earlier. The next day my friend walked in and said "I just got back from California where I got rebirthed. You'll have to do it." We were about to leave for New England for a retreat, and there was a training center for rebirthing in Walton, New York, so we decided to go there for me to get rebirthed. It was quite a story, getting there, with our car breaking down and this and that—various little resistances to being there—but when I arrived, Steven Star was there as the trainer, and he is now my husband and the father of Mela Noel.

S: He was your first rebirther?

R: He was my very first rebirther. So he talked to me about birth trauma and about babies being conscious at birth, and everything he said confirmed what was growing in my own mind, that people could remember their birth. It made absolute sense to me. I understood why the birth in 1968 was so

121

traumatic. One reason is that I had been born cesarean, and so when I was giving birth it felt wrong to me to be having a baby that way. I felt that it should have been cesarean, and indeed, at the end of that delivery, the doctor said "Boy, if I had known this we would have done the cesarean," and that had felt correct to me. As Steven was talking to me about rebirthing and birth trauma, all the pieces of the puzzle fell together and made sense.

S: How long before you got pregnant the second time did you start rebirthing?

R: I started rebirthing in 1977. The son that I had in 1968 had died by drowning in 1972, so in 1977 when I started rebirthing, I healed a lot of the sadness and grief over his death. I realized that life is eternal, whether we leave our bodies or not, and I had a real sense of completion with that. I had thought I wouldn't have any more children. I thought that I had so many things to do in the world, so many ways I wanted to serve people, that I should not be having children. It just didn't seem right. As I healed my own birth through rebirthing, and felt more and more complete with my son's death and with healing my own inner child, I noticed there were more and more children in my environment, and that I felt more and more comfortable about it.

In 1978 I met Steven for the second time at the Rebirther's Convention in Colorado, and that time we could no longer deny that we really loved each other a lot. The attraction we felt for each other a year earlier was still there, so we decided to be a couple and get married. It was at that time when I had this experience of healing in myself, where I felt totally complete, whether I ever had another child or not. I sensed that I was complete, whether I got married or didn't get married, whether I had a baby or didn't have a baby, that no matter what were the external things in my life, I had a sense of inner completion. After that realization I had a tremendous amount of freedom in my life, because I didn't have these needs.

Occasionally in the past I had thought "Oh, you should have a baby, women should have babies, you shouldn't miss this experience, your parents would love to have a grandchild," and all these things, and after that I just felt great. It didn't matter to me one way or the other, and that was when I began noticing children in my environment. We moved to Austin, and all of a sudden I was rebirthing seven midwives.

They began inviting me to births, to assist them with women who were having problems during labor because they had thoughts or fears they couldn't release. They also invited me to work with women on breathing and affirmations to release fears that were going on in their labors. So I had quite a bit of experience with births and was able to heal my idea that birth had to be painful, or traumatic, or long, or uncomfortable. About the same time Steven and I began, both of us, sensing a presence that would be with us occasionally, just a spiritual presence. A lot of times it seemed to me that it was the same being as the little boy I'd had.

S: Really?

R: Of course you say "Well, is it or isn't it?" But it really didn't matter to us. We knew there was a being with us that was very loving and we felt this kind of communication going on.

S: What kind of communication? *Asking* you to be the parents?

R: There was definitely the question of whether we wanted to allow this being to come through us. Did we want to have that child?

We looked at the idea for about a year before we actually decided to conceive and allow this being to come through. The year was very cleansing for Steve and me. He cleansed a lot of his thoughts about children. (Can we afford them? What will we do? and How?). You know, we wanted to be wonderful parents. We want to be the best we can to assist a being in being here.

123

S: How did you do a cleansing process? I understand you started clearing the thoughts that made you nervous about pregnancy and the babies. This cleansing process—are you talking about rebirthing?

R: Well, at that point, Steve began a completion process that I had perhaps completed earlier in a different way. All his family thoughts started coming up. Anytime you put a new idea into your consciousness it brings up anything unlike it. So you put the idea in there—Let's think about conceiving a baby—and every thought comes up, from what your grandfather said, to your mother, your father, and so on. That happened for Steve, and for me too. We looked at those thoughts, and chose those that were in harmony with our highest desires about children and pregnancy.

S: So you took quite a while before conception to prepare yourself.

R: Right. On a physical level we had already started a cleansing process that year, doing different kinds of fasting. We did lots of fasting that year. We did lots of building up our nutrition and exercising. I've been doing martial arts for a couple of years and Steven was into really mastering his body. I feel that we were being guided the whole time in preparation for this, and that's what I mean.

S: Very good. So is there anything else you did to prepare yourself for conception?

R: Well, we had a beautiful time playing with the idea of having a child, just clearing our fears and our thoughts about our relationship and about what we wanted to be like for the child. We did lots of rebirthing because we are rebirthers and we do a lot of that anyway. I continued to be around birth a lot, and so did Steven.

S: So then were you taking birth control during that period?

R: No, I hadn't used birth control for about four or five years in the conventional sense. I did use a diaphragm occasionally, but mainly for three years I just used my thoughts, and would tell beings not to come through me: "I'm not ready and Steve's not ready." That worked.

S: That's interesting. How did you finally feel ready? Did you just know it one day? You woke up and suddenly knew "Okay, now I'm ready to have this being come through me?"

R: That was about how it happened.

S: And Steve had the same timing?

R: It was in February, 1980. We both woke up after this process of . . . all of a sudden we looked at each other and we said, "Let's have this child." And we both felt just very joyous because we knew it was right and it was complete. Oh, I know what happened. I was writing an article for this magazine called *Mothering* on divine childbirth and rebirthing. I was sitting at my typewriter one night and all of a sudden I realized there were no more blocks in my consciousness to having this child come through, and I felt that there were no more blocks in Steve's consciousness, although he wasn't even in the room. It's as if I felt our two thoughts merge. I felt at that moment we were pregnant, even though we had not had sex. The next morning is when we woke up and looked at each other and said "Let's have this baby." Of course we already had started it.

S: And so you went through an experience where you consciously felt conception happening.

125

R: Right, at a mental level. That's when I understood the Immaculate Conception. At least my understanding is that you have to create things in your mind first (at the thought level we were very much pregnant). I imagine that if you could put a lot of energy in that thought you could manifest pregnancy without necessarily having sex.

S: There are cultures where they've done that—the Trobriand Islands. It's very interesting.

R: It was a powerful realization for me that you can have so much thought that you can manifest a being just by your thought, without necessarily having to go through the body. I realized that very profoundly. I almost felt that I could create the baby right there in my hands within five minutes. That thought really scared me because I said "God, how would I explain this?" I'd walk in tomorrow morning and say, "Oh, look. Here's a baby." Here's our child. I didn't tell you we were pregnant." Well, I decided that having a baby in the conventional manner was probably just as good, and I thought we'd do it that way.

S: It gives you time to get ready. So then you experienced actually creating it that morning?

R: Well, no. That morning we decided it, and then we were very happy and so we called Steve's parents in Oregon and said "We just want you to know that we've gotten very clear, we're going to have a child." They were delighted. We were planning to go out to dinner that night with my parents to the best French restaurant in San Antonio, which I love very much, a wonderful place. And then we were going to a Valentine dance with my parents. During dinner we told them we had decided to have a child and thought we'd conceive in May. That was our plan. I'm their only child, so they were thrilled to be having another grandchild. We went to the dance and had a marvelous time—a lot of fun and a lot of love. I danced with my father and it was just very sweet, a very beautiful feeling among all of us. So then we went to my parents' house and we made love and we conceived.

S: Right that night?

R: Even though our minds had been saying we'd get pregnant in May, because we thought that was more appropriate and it means the baby will come such and such, we had it all worked out; however, in our hearts, we had already decided that this was it.

S: In your parents' house you conceived?

R: Right.

S: That's very interesting, isn't it?

R: I guess at some level we knew we would conceive that night, but our minds were trying to do this little control number.

S: When did you realize you were pregnant?

R: During that whole next month. I first thought that I really was pregnant in March, about four weeks later, when we were at a certified rebirthers' meeting in Santa Barbara and I was feeling really weird. I was dreaming about babies and just a different energy was going on. Somebody said to me "Do you think you're pregnant?" and I said "Oh, no. We're not going to conceive until May." When we came home and I continued to have this strange feeling we realized yes, we are pregnant, and that put Steve through . . . I realized why we had set up this May thing, because it helped Steve especially to process his feelings about being in control. He went through some hard days thinking "How could this pregnancy happen without my consent?" His ego went through some difficulty and he really had to look at that. It brought up feelings for him about being forced and about not having any choice in the matter. Not that he was blaming me, it was like he was blaming God or something. I, too, felt the reason we'd set it up that way was so that we could clear any of this stuff. So during this time I felt really strange in my body, with lots of cross energy, and I felt a little tired, a little bit sick; and I felt that the baby was with us on the outside, but it wasn't inside yet. We'd gone through this for about a week and finally I told Steve "Okay, Steve, if you really don't want to have the baby now, I'm willing to have an abortion, because I want you to know that you have a choice."

Well, when I said that to him, it changed everything, because I was giving back his power in the matter. That changed everything and he was totally ready to surrender.

S: He let go completely, right?

R: Yes. During the weeks all of this was going on we felt the presence of a baby.

S: Waiting for you to get clear?

R: Right. It was not going to rush in without our permission. When Steve changed his mind I remember I was in the bathtub rebirthing myself, and I just sat up and said, "Steven, come in here," and we both looked at each other and started crying. I started talking to the baby's spirit, who was on the outside, and I said "Forgive me for thinking that a ten- or twelve-week difference is a big deal. Forgive me for being so arrogant. I just surrendered. Steve and I looked at each other and realized how silly it was to be having this huge debate over twelve weeks, or whatever it was. We both cried and we welcomed the baby into our hearts and into our lives. That next weekend I was leading a training on relationships—I was maybe six weeks pregnant—and all of a sudden I felt the spirit of the baby choose to come into the body of the baby at that time.

S: What was that like?

R: It was a day-long process. I told Jackie, who was co-leading the workshop, "I'm just going to lie down right now." It was beautiful being there with everyone. I went through this process of receiving the baby's spirit into my body and it felt like one of the highest meditations I have ever done. I've done some silent meditation retreats, and at the end of ten or twelve days not speaking, just being and breathing and sitting and walking, I felt very close to God and very peaceful and very harmonious. That was the feeling I had that whole day. It was like I was enveloped in total safety and love and white light, and I felt the baby's spirit hug me, like every molecule of mine was being hugged by the molecules of this being.

S: Oh, that's beautiful.

R: It was just luscious and wonderful. Then after that I felt the spirit center in the baby's body within me.

S: Physically or mentally?

R: Physically.

S: And how far along were you at that moment?

R: Six or seven weeks.

S: At six or seven weeks you felt the baby's spirit enter? You totally accepted the pregnancy at that moment?

R: Right.

S: That was very beautiful. What was the first trimester of your pregnancy like?

R: Well, that was the first seven weeks of it. I had some feelings of what they traditionally call morning sickness. I threw up a few times, maybe six times in that whole three months.

S: Could you tell what triggered you to have the morning sickness?

R: Yes. It was nothing compared to my first pregnancy. Then I was sick a lot, and I lost 12 pounds in the first three months. This time I felt a little low, so I took frequent naps. I realized that for me morning sickness was just a period for adjusting to the increase of spirit in my body. It was just surrendering and surrendering and surrendering to more spirit being with me all the time.

S: I have this theory that morning sickness signals the releasing of any resistance you had to more life. The extra life urge pushes out anything unlike itself.

R: At a physical, emotional spiritual level, it's just letting life be there. When I would be feeling a little off I would just get in the bathtub and breathe, and I would welcome life and welcome the baby. I was learning to change my routine. I mean before then I was going twenty places a day and doing all kinds of projects. Now I was surrendering to the project of creating a baby in my body, and setting other projects aside. It was a mental process for me to surrender to my project of having a baby. I gave myself permission to take naps and to take walks and to breathe in the bathtub. I tell people that, if they haven't learned to nurture themselves before they have a baby, they will definitely learn to do it while they're pregnant and when they have a child, because when you have children you need to nurture yourself even more. You need to see how much you deserve nurturing. That process of learning to nurture myself even more began in the first trimester.

S: And you rebirthed yourself a lot?

R: Yes.

S: Wet rebirthing?

R: Right.

S: In your bathtub?

R: In the bathtub. I would do connected breathing sometimes it seemed 24 hours a day.

S: I can imagine it helped a lot, and kept you from having heavy morning sickness, didn't it?

R: It did.

S: And was your husband rebirthing himself during the first three months?

R: Yes. He was truly a pregnant father. After my first child I had a divorce and I thought "Oh, men just cannot understand pregnancy. If I ever get pregnant again I'm just going to be around women, who understand it." I had this thought that men just can't get it. Steven proved that wrong. I was real proud of myself for creating a husband who realized that he was pregnant too. He definitely was, and he went through a lot of similar thoughts and feelings in preparing for the baby and he was right there with me.

S: Great. Did he rebirth you too, or did you rebirth yourself.

R: Both. I rebirthed myself, but he was my main rebirther during pregnancy.

S: Then you started growing and feeling something. Tell me about the second trimester.

R: Well, about April or May there was a shift in energy. I compare the nine months of pregnancy to a rebirthing: the first three months are this buildup of energy and it might feel a little chaotic; the next three months I describe as a plateau of total joy and extreme aliveness and energy—you feel that you can do anything; and then the last three months are like the end of a rebirthing session when all that energy and that plateau of high spiritual harmony and peace is just releasing through your whole body, and with that energy the baby comes out. Basically, that's how I see the nine months.

The second three months for me . . . . In May Steven and my friend Jack were both rebirthing me in a beautiful tub at a friend's house, and all of a sudden I stood up and I just . . . I realized I had a little belly there for the first time. It was like someone had punched a button and I was off of the first three months and into the second, and I felt really high and wonderful. I felt *pregnant*. I could feel the baby moving around at about 12 weeks. I had a definite sense that she was a girl. So did Steve, and in that rebirthing with Steven and Jack I had this message from her that her name was supposed to mean "celebration." From that rebirthing on I had a lot of energy. I decided to go see Leonard Orr and Jeannie Carr, whom I hadn't seen in quite a while, so I went to California and visited with them. It was great. I went to the baths and hiked around, and I felt very high and very healthy. I felt that I was glowing for miles.

S: To Campbell Hot Springs?

R: Yes. When I came back here, Steven was going through the same things that, I feel, his parents probably went through when they were pregnant. I, too, was having thoughts come up and I didn't have any idea where they came from. The only place I could figure out is that they came from thoughts my parents were having while they were

132

pregnant with me, and I realized that this whole pregnancy was a cleansing of our experience of our being inside our mothers' wombs, and what was happening during that time in our families. Steve and I went through a couple of hard months during June and July. I was feeling better and better—just as if I could climb a mountain and do all kinds of things, and he was feeling pretty low. Steve had a lot of feelings of separation and fear then, so it took us a couple of months to really clear that out and come together. For us it was a healing of a lot of past thoughts. I felt like being with people and having fun, and he was feeling more and more like crawling in a hole. He wanted to stay in his room and not get out of bed, so we spent some time there. We just had to keep trusting that everything was fine and that we would come together; about July or August that was over for him.

S: What helped the most to get through that?

R: What helped me the most was to continue to show what I felt was best for me even though he was feeling rotten. At first, I would think "Oh well, you better not be too happy today, you better just hang your head and be a little sad, because *he* is." Finally I got that what pleasures me is going to heal *him* faster than anything else. and what pleasures him is going to heal *us* faster than anything else. What started changing our relationship was when I said "Steve, I love and support you and I want you to do what is best for you, and I'm going to do the same for me." So I started going out to luncheons or shopping with my friends, and I'd have a great time. I would feel sadness about what was going on with him, but basically I was taking care of myself. I felt that, by not buying into his feelings I enabled him to get out of it faster.

S: You didn't match energies with where he was.

R: Right. It was a big lesson for me, because in the past I would have thought that if your husband's sad and upset you've got to go along with that. I chose not to do that, and I trusted that our relationship would make it even through this.

S: And then that just passed for him at the end of the second trimester?

R: Well, it was during the Rebirthers' Convention. At the convention Steve gave up a big chunk of his old pattern. He allowed himself to be a first-class person—citizen, teacher and healer—after that. Before that, he'd had a personal law about not being good enough, and that he's always wrong, or there's something wrong with him, and he was really attached to that. He got a lot of mileage out of not being good enough. He got to blame people and do this and that, and he really gave it up. He saw how it was kind of a family tradition to be this rebellious person. He really wasn't owning his first-class abilities. During the Convention that August I felt Steve drop his negative personal laws.

S: I remember how beautiful you looked. You were quite pregnant then. What month was that?

R: That was the beginning of the last trimester. During those middle months I had done a lot of teaching about pregnancy and prenatal thoughts and how your relationship with that baby is going on all the time. We kept clearing with the baby constantly while we were pregnant. If we were having a fight we would clear with her. "Look, we're feeling these feelings, this is going on, but we want you to know we love you and we love each other." We would explain to the baby what was going on with us and that it was okay. I mean ultimately everything was fine; we were just releasing old feelings and thoughts.

S: So you began the bonding right away. Did you speak to the baby all through the pregnancy?

134

R: Yes, and before we conceived.

S: Even before conception you started speaking to it. I think that's very important with an ideal birth, don't you?

R: I think so, absolutely.

S: I think that's the key thing.

R: I felt more sensuous and beautiful than ever in the third trimester. In the seventh month I was still feeling very high and extroverted. I felt I had a lot to share with people; being pregnant opened up my mental filing cabinet on pregnancy and all these thoughts came out that I'd heard when I was a child. You know, when a woman was pregnant she'd kind of hide her body, and stay at home, and I remember my mother saying "We are going to a party, but so-and-so's not coming. She's pregnant, and she feels fat and ugly."

S: That wasn't your experience.

R: No. I realized that pregnancy is a time of increased aliveness and sensuality—increased awareness of your body and the beauty of it—and you'd really have to do a lot to tie down that energy and aliveness. I used to think all pregnant women were fat and ugly, and this time I didn't think that at all, and I had lots of fun.

S: Just a shift in attitude.

R: Right. I could see the whole cultural thing about it.

S: You just didn't go into agreement with the group mind, isn't that the difference? You certainly didn't look fat and ugly.

R: I had forgotten about these thoughts many years ago, and so I just "rewrote" them. I began to talk about the beauty of pregnancy and pregnant women, and people were changing their minds—because there was a lot of thought out there in the universe that pregnancy is dull and uninteresting.

S: I'm glad you proved that wrong.

R: It was fun.

S: How about the third trimester? Did you have any physical problems? And what about sex during this period?

R: When we came home from the Convention that August I noticed a definite shift in my energy. Instead of being extroverted, I was doing remodeling and painting, getting the house ready, and I became more inner-directed. I felt the changes going on in my body and I felt more like nesting. I was preparing our space for the baby, and I was preparing myself mentally. I rebirthed myself every single day during the last two and one-half months before she came.

S: In water?

R: In the bathtub with a snorkel. It was just exquisite. I felt a lot of telepathic messages from the baby. In earlier rebirths I had got the message from her "I like rebirthing—do it some more."

S: She liked it when you breathed.

R: She loved it. So the last two and one-half months I had a massage 2 or 3 times a week and I rebirthed myself every single day. Also, there's a common thought that during the last three months it gets crowded and uncomfortable for the baby and that's why they decide to come out. I didn't like that thought, so I decided that what happens the last three months is the baby gets grounded and really feels safe. In those first few months the baby is so free in there. I had this

136

memory of being in my mother's womb. I was so little and there was so much space that I was just floating around in all this freedom. I would roll over this and roll over that. In the middle three months it was more balanced, and the last three months I got a sense of groundedness, of being hugged. You get a sense of safety. It's not crowded—there's plenty of space. You get this sense of "Oh, I'm really loved, I'm really held securely and nestled and loved." You've explored and mastered that space, so you decide "I'm ready to explore somewhere else." That's my thought about what happens. While our baby was mastering her space inside, I was mastering and releasing some of the last fears that I had about the birth, and we were still debating at that time about underwater birth.

S: When did you start thinking about that?

R: We started thinking about it from Day 1.

S: Let's talk about that in a minute. I want to get back to how you felt about sex during your pregnancy, and especially during the last trimester.

R: During the middle trimester I felt an abundance of sexual energy. The last three months I felt a little calmer, but I enjoyed sex very much, and we had sex I think a day or two before Mela was born. We communicated with her about sexuality and about our loving each other and what sex was about for us and we felt like she was definitely a part of it. She was right there in the middle and I felt that she really felt loved. In our research since then, we've discovered a lot of people have guilt about their parents having sex when they were in the womb. The father thought he could hurt the baby by having sex, or the mother thought it was wrong to have sex but she was doing it anyway, and the baby in the womb picked up a lot of guilt. So we talked to the baby about sexuality.

S: You included it in the sexual experience.

R: Right.

S: Certainly we've seen in books now coming out that sexual attitudes start in the womb. You can see why—the baby is picking up everything you're feeling. Did you have any problems toward the end of the third trimester? Physically?

R: No. I was one of the healthiest pregnant women that this doctor ever saw. I went to a medical doctor twice during my pregnancy. He is a doctor who no longer delivers babies, but he's delivered probably over ten thousand. The midwives I work with send their clients to him for prenatal care. I went to him and had blood work done. I had a very good hematocrit and hemoglobin, very good iron, calcium, all of that. He said I was one of the healthiest pregnant women he had ever seen and what did I do? I said "Well, I breathe a lot." All I take is Spirolina." Spirolina is an algae plankton that has lots of everything in it. I took extra vitamin C and extra calcium, and that's all. I felt very healthy and he confirmed it. It was also good for me to see him because my midwives have participated in over 1,000 births, but this man had done over 10,000. The instant he placed his hands on my belly to feel the position of the baby I could just feel that experience. He said he thought I could have a wonderful homebirth and he was delighted I was doing that. He was very nice. So the last few months I felt good. I did a lot of walking and I had massages, so I kept myself on top of it. If I'd go for five or six days without a massage I would want one, because I was getting bigger and bigger and it just felt good in my back and legs.

Steve and I were also doing childbirth classes with our midwives and so we were doing certain exercises. We would practice different things. We would visualize the baby being born. Since I had been born cesarean, I wanted to be sure I put into my mind the awareness that having a baby come out through my vagina was appropriate. I'd get these books, and try to figure out exactly how a baby comes out. A woman's anatomy is not just a straight line from the cervix out. There's actually a little S-curve and the baby has to kind of spiral out. I remember trying to figure out exactly how the baby's head is when they turn it this way and when they turn it that way and how they do this, and I finally got in my mind exactly how a baby is born. The chin is flexed and the head is down and the baby makes a little turn to come out. Steve and I would visualize it and "walk through" it. I'd say to the baby "This is how you're going to have your head, it'll work just like this." During this last trimester we also met with the people whom we had invited to attend our birth.

S: Did you have a midwife all the way through the pregnancy that you *relied on?*

R: Well, I had three midwives whom I had been rebirthing for over a year. I saw them a lot because they're some of my best friends, so they examined me whenever I asked them to. They would develop a relationship with the baby when they were examining me and they always talked to the baby.

S: Okay, go ahead. You were talking about the group that was going to be at the birth.

R: Right. The last three months is when we prepared ourselves as a group. We had five or six gatherings of everyone who will be attending our birth.

S: You mean you started having meetings ahead of time?

R: Right. We had three midwives and several friends. Our friend, Arthur Kidd, was at our birth to do massage. Elizabeth, who is the mother of two children and a close friend was invited to come. Several other friends all had tasks to do around the house. We knew we were going to be photographing and videotaping the birth. We didn't know yet that it would definitely be under water, but we knew it would be wonderful and we wanted to record it.

S: What did you do at these meetings? Just talk about feelings?

R: Our first meeting was very intense. Because everybody had so many fears. I suggested doing this process "A fear or expectation I have about this birth is . . ." Everyone had tons of expectations and fears. I had been rebirthing the midwives for over a year so they'd been kind of my clients and now here I was being their client. There was a lot of stuff about approval and wanting to do well. Just everybody wanting it to be right. You know, here I am, this wonderful rebirther, this supposedly New Age, enlightened, divine being, and what if the birth was a mess?

S: Oh, that was everybody's worst fear.

R: You know, how would we explain that? So we cleared all of that. Basically we decided the birth was going to be perfect and there was nothing we could do about that. It was very good. We really got off a lot of ego thoughts. The next time we got together I made a tape where everyone who was going to be present at the birth talked to the baby. I still have this tape.

They'd walk up and touch the baby and say "What I want you to know about my being at your birth is that I'm there to support you and that I love you and that I love your mother, too, you know."

Steve talked to the baby and, oh God, we were in tears. I talked to the baby. We told the baby everything we wanted her to know about our presence at her birth. We had cleared ourselves with the baby, and we felt that Mela definitely approved of everyone who was at the birth and she had a relationship with them and they had a relationship with her.

Afterwards we sat in a circle and chanted and sang and I recorded that. A few days later you called me and said "Just

140

remember this affirmation: My mind is God's mind and my body is God's body and my spirit is God's Spirit." You were studying the *Course in Miracles,* and you said "This is it." So I started chanting that. It was wonderful. I recorded on the tape my highest thoughts about labor and birth. I thought it was the best gift I gave myself.

Then Peter Gonzales arrived about two weeks before Mela was born. He's a professional photographer, professonal soccer player and a rebirther. His birthday is June 15, mine is June 16, and he was in our first One-Year Seminar here in Austin. We feel very close and love him a lot. He was to be the photographer of this birth. He is one of the most sensitive people I could ever want to meet.

In the last two weeks we spent a lot of time together. We'd go out in the hill country of Texas which, in October, is just gorgeous; we'd have picnics and he did a lot of photographing, which we have in our slide show of Mela's birth. During those last weeks I felt really loved and appreciated. Everyone took care of me. They'd feed me and take me places—oh, it was really very luxurious. Everyone would gather here in the evenings, someone would fix dinner, and we'd talk. There was nothing to clear, there was only our willingness to serve this baby.

S: That sounds wonderful. Now I'd like to talk a little bit about the underwater birth, how you'd heard about it, how you finally decided to do it. When did you first hear about it?

R: A couple of years before I had Mela, I saw a TV program with little babies swimming in this plexiglas tank. It mentioned Russian's underwater babies. I had missed the beginning, and I probably missed the end, but I'll never forget that picture. That picture was in my mind and when I got pregnant Steve said "You know, the Russians have been having babies underwater."

We read an article in the paper that said Russians are having babies underwater to create superintelligent beings that can master space. So we began talking about it right away.

In May when I went to Campbell Hot Springs there was a woman whom I had known in Oklahoma who was pregnant, and she had decided she was going to have her baby in the hot springs there at Campbell's.

S: She had seen the same film?

R: I'm not sure. Then, when we were at the Rebirthers' Convention in August, we met Patrick and Jia Lighthouse, who were rebirthers in San Diego. Their baby was due about the same time as ours and they were planning to have an underwater birth in a fiberglass tub. They had also heard something about it and they had talked to someone who knew someone else who had her baby underwater, they thought. So I said "Well, I really want to know about it. Let us know about it." We liked the idea intellectually. It seemed logical for the baby, who has been in the amniotic sac for nine months to come through the birth canal into relaxing water, and to have a few minutes to release any stress of the birth canal, and just to feel safe, before coming into the air. I researched the umbilical cord and the oxygen supply, and I felt that, as long as the placenta was attached and the umbilical cord was pulsing strongly, the baby would get plenty of oxygen. Then Patrick and Jia told us they had learned that babies in the amniotic sac actually swallow water and spit it out. So, I figured, well, if she's not breathing in the amniotic sac why would she breath when she came out in water. She would probably just swallow and spit out like she did in the amniotic sac, if anything. So we felt that doing the birth underwater was very safe and loving. My main resistance to it was that I had had a son who drowned, and I felt this was the same spirit, and I thought, God, am I supposed to do this?

S: Have one child go out underwater and one child come in.

R: That's right, and so one time I rebirthed myself in the

tub and I said, "Okay, God, I'll visualize this thing happening underwater."

S: . . . being delivered underwater.

R: I'm going to visualize *myself* being born underwater. Mentally I did that, and the feeling I had when I imagined my head coming out into the water was one of liquid love; those are the words that came to me. The water presented pure love and, of course, I had my father's hands there catching me, and love everywhere, and the water felt exquisite. It felt great and I still had some resistances to it. So finally I wrote a letter to Babaji in the Himalayas. I said "Dear Babaji, I'm getting tired of trying to figure this birth out and trying to control this thing and wondering if it's going to be this way and that way. I just want to surrender this birth to you. If it's appropriate for me to have an underwater birth, just let me know and let it be easy." I felt I had to do clearing with my midwives, because this was a new thing for them, and society, and everybody. I mean it was a new thought, underwater birth. I still hadn't decided for sure and we didn't have a tub or anything.

S: I find it interesting that you wrote that letter to Babaji, which I didn't know about. I took Mela's picture to Babaji right after the birth to ask him to bless it. I remember I said to him "Babaji, I want you to bless this child. It was born underwater." He got this incredible joy and when he saw her picture he started laughing and I couldn't figure out what he was laughing at.

R: Well, I wrote him, and it worked, because that's when I really let go of trying to control things. I just let go and started having fun. The last few weeks I just had a blast and Peter photographed it. Mela was already past due and we still hadn't decided for sure. I didn't have a clear sign.

143

S: So you prepared to have the baby in a bed. When did you start thinking about the tub?

R: Well, I was a little nervous about the tub, but I knew that if there was going to be a way, it would be easy, because I'd asked this of Babaji and thought I'd get it. Then Patrick and Jia called (this was already past Mela's due date), and they had just had Jeremy underwater and they told us all about the birth. Steve and I were both on the phone listening to them and all of a sudden this white light just flew into me and I felt *this is it, it's underwater!* I *knew* it absolutely, with not one doubt in any molecule of my being. That was the sign.

S: That was while you were talking to them on the phone?

R: Right. Somehow in talking with them I got certainty on it. That was a Sunday. Steve said "Well, in Walton we used to do rebirthing in a cattle trough and it was perfect. It was a good size, it was this length and that length; he kept talking about the cattle trough and how perfect it was, so I said "Come on, let's go buy one." So Monday morning we went . . .

S: You were overdue and buying a cattle trough? It's kind of funny. It's Texas-style, right?

R: Yes. So we went to the farmer's Feed and Supply and got the cattle trough. At first we thought maybe we should rent it. What'll we do with a cattle trough?

S: How much is a cattle trough?

R: $100. We said we wanted to rent a cattle trough and they said "Oh are you going to have a beer party? I said, "No, we're going to have our baby in here." Oh, they jumped back. You could tell they had never thought about anything like that.

144

S: Probably haven't recovered since!

R: Then they got worried. "We can't rent it to you. What if . . . I mean, could we be liable for something?" Steve said, "We could use it for rebirthing, you know," so we decided to buy it. So we bought the trough. We painted it on Monday (non-toxic rust-proof white paint because we didn't want it gray and we were going to be taking photographs) and dried it with heaters on Tuesday. Wednesday I had the baby.

S: So Mela just waited around for you to get this ready, it seems.

R: I knew Tuesday night, November 4. The tub was out there drying, everything was ready. When we knew it was going to be underwater, we called our midwives and they called Patrick and Jia and asked all the questions they wanted to ask. We put a salt solution in the water, we got everything figured out, and everybody got it together. It was election night, November 4. We had just taken a walk and I was watching Ronald Reagan's speech on television when I got the thought of coming out. So I said "This is it." I was very excited. Everyone had just left the house—it was just Steve and me—and I went in the bathroom, got in the tub and started rebirthing myself. The phone rang and it was you.

S: Oh, that was good timing.

R: And you just, I don't know what, you just called. . . .

S: I told you I had to go to India or something. I think that's one of the reasons. I just felt you were having your labor. It was time I guess.

R: And I think I said "Well, this is it. I'm in the bathtub. Call tomorrow, we'll probably have a baby." I felt very blessed that you called, and somebody else called right after

145

you, I think maybe Jack. That was about 8 o'clock, and then we went to bed. I was feeling the energy, it was definitely early labor, and I was thrilled. I thought it was the best thing in the world to have this baby. I woke up about 3 or 4 in the morning and called the midwives. One thing I forgot that I want to share happened before this. The week before Mela came I had to go through a process of letting go of being pregnant, and I feel that every pregnant woman has to go through this.

S: Because it's such a glorious time and you have to give up all that.

R: Because I had to be willing not to be pregnant. One night, a few nights before, I started crying. "Steven," I said, "if I have this baby I'm not going to be pregnant anymore."

S: It's interesting, you know.

R: It just hit me that I couldn't have the baby and stay pregnant, which I didn't really want to do, but I realized that I was saying goodbye to my relationship of knowing **Mela** on the inside. I felt I needed to do some releasing to let her come out and let our relationship expand, so I said goodbye to my pregnant body. I loved it and blessed it and then I was willing to have the baby come out.

S: That's good. Now you're in labor and you're calling the midwives at 3 A.M.

R: Three in the morning. I called my midwives and they were very excited, called everybody. Peter and Arthur, and everyone came over between 3 and 5. Steve and I were just in bed. Steve, I just loved him so much, he was so sweet and so right there. I mean he wasn't wiped out or frightened or anything.

146

S: It's great to have him right there as opposed to a hospital birth, isn't it?

R: Yeah. He had his beads and he was going *"Om Namaha Shivai"* (chanting), blessing the baby and blessing me. So I was in labor and that was it. Another thing that happened in my preparation for labor was, a few days before, my friend walked in and said "Well, how do you feel about intense pain?" She just walked in and said that to me and it's like it just knocked me for a loop. I definitely had a position that I didn't want to experience pain, or what I thought was pain, so when she just came right out and used the word *pain* instead of intense energy or intense something else, I had to think, what I was going to do if I felt like some of this was painful. It was very healing for me, because I said "Okay, what is pain?" I realized that pain is a thought and it comes from fear. It's either fear that the sensation you're experiencing is going to kill you, or it's going to hurt you irreparably, or it's going to last longer than you do.

S: Right at bottom is always death. Leonard used to tell us that death is the stronghold of all fear.

R: Well, I looked at those things and I said well, I know I'm not dying, because I don't plan to do that at all. I know that my body is made to give birth and it's going to work and I know that any sensation I might think is pain is not going to last forever.

S: Good. So that helped you a lot in labor?

R: I knew that in labor whatever I experienced was okay, and if my mind came up with pain I would just look at that and say I'm going to make it. I just cleared those negative thoughts. So my labor started and the energy was building up and I was feeling very high and very happy and very

147

blessed. I had always thought that I wanted my birth, the whole thing, to be about 12 hours. I didn't want it to be 2 hours or 20 minutes. I wanted to take pleasure in the process and so, in my mind, 12 hours of labor seemed about right. I ended up having 17, which I can explain later. I know now why that happened.

S: So you really *wanted* to have 12 hours of labor. You looked forward to that?

R: I mean I felt that that was my ideal amount of time. That's what came up for me, because I wanted to take pleasure in it and I wanted Mela to have plenty of time. I've seen adults who were born real fast and it wasn't necessarily the greatest. They didn't have time for a lot of the processes that I think needed some time to occur. Each process of the labor does different things for the baby, for the baby's body and the brain and everything else. So, for me, I didn't want any 10-minute stuff or 2-hour stuff, I wanted some time to experience and go with it. And to enjoy myself. See, I had nine people waiting on me hand and foot!

S: Were you in this room?

R: No, this is where the tub was, in my office, but I was in my bedroom and the living room and the backyard. I enjoyed the idea, and everyone was really so wonderful. Cathy examined me early that morning, and I was 4 centimeters dilated. Ten centimeters is complete dilation, where the baby's head can come out. I would just breathe and be with Steve and relax into the energy and into the feelings of the birth. Then I got in the bathtub and spent a couple of hours in there. I had a blast! Here was Peter taking my picture as I was sitting in the bathtub and everyone was standing there looking at me and I said "Peter, hand me the camera," so I sat in the bathtub and took a picture of everybody from my viewpoint. Having everybody surrounding me and handing me juice and loving me and laughing was really fun.

148

S: How about your contractions? Were they . . . .

R: Well, I called them *expansions*.

S: Oh good. You changed the name. That makes more sense.

R: Because in my mind what is happening is that the muscles are contracting so the cervix can expand.

S: Right, that is the purpose of the labor.

R: Right. I thought, being so smart, I'm going to focus on expansion.

S: That's good. It helped, didn't it.

R: Yes. I'd say "Oh, I'm having a great expansion right now." When you have one, you can see the belly contracting up almost round instead of kind of elliptical, and then the cervix would expand. They were coming every 3 to 4 minutes, whatever, and I would love them to give in to them, and they actually felt good. Then the energy increased, in the part of labor called transition, which is commonly the time of the most intensity. That's when the cervix is expanding those last two centimeters. This is when women have thoughts that they're dying, they're not going to make it, this is too much, I'm going to quit and go home. When you read textbooks on birth, they say we know a woman's in transition when she starts talking like this.

S: That's supposed to be the hardest part.

R: Several times I did have thoughts come up about—am I going to make this? Is this going to be all right? And I would say "Of course, it is." It was so clear to me where those thoughts came from. Those negative thoughts had nothing to do with present time. They had to do with memory—memories of my earlier labor, memories from my own birth, and so on. I would just look at each one, take a deep breath, let it go, and relax into the sensation. What I did in my labor (which is not necessarily the way labor has been taught) was to *go down into my body* even more. Sometimes in childbirth classes they teach women to leave their bodies more (in other words, to separate themselves from the sensation). Well, my whole training in rebirthing and self-improvement has taught me to go into the energy—that when you relax into pain it becomes pleasure if you totally surrender. I felt that rolfing and body work and rebirthing were fantastic preparations for this. To me the ideal way to do labor was, not to run away from it, but to go into it, so I was very inner-directed towards the last part of my labor. I wasn't horsing around with people any more, and having conversation, I was just riding . . .

S: Were you still in bed?

R: Oh, I had been different places. Most of the early labor I was in bed with Steve. Towards the last part of labor and transition I was in the bathtub and I was walking around. I would stand up and hang on to Steve, with my arms around his shoulders, and bend over, because when the baby comes down there's a point where the baby is heading exactly towards the sacrum. See, that's that curve the baby has to make. It goes toward your sacrum and makes a little turn, and so there was a part where there was a lot of energy going towards my sacrum. For me to bend over and let the baby's weight drop towards the floor would relieve my sacrum; I'd have people lightly stroke the small of my back and it felt great. It would just take the energy and disperse it. So I did walking around and bending over and breathing and just surrendering down into my body. I felt so safe in my body. The last couple of centimeters though, I felt I didn't know exactly what was what, so I'd just relax and breathe. Right at the end of my transition, I was sitting on my bed and somebody said "Let's put Rima's tape on," the tape I had made, so for these last couple of centimeters . . .

S: How many hours are you into labor now?

R: Probably 12.

S: You have already had 12 hours of labor?

R: Well, active labor had started around 3 in the morning, and this was probably about 3 or 4 in the afternoon.

S: And everybody had stayed through the whole labor.

R: Oh, yeah.

S: How did you know when to get into the tub?

R: People were doing different things. They were cooking and eating and getting me things, and it was like a party. . .

S: It was like a celebration.

R: Right. It was a family celebration; it was just very high. I loved having all that energy in the house, because some of my closest friends were putting their best into this—their best thoughts. They weren't in the kitchen thinking, oh, this is crummy and she's not going to make it. They were in the kitchen thinking, this is wonderful, and they were having scenes from their own births come up for them and breathing it out—and you know, it was wonderful.

S: It sounds like everybody was rebirthing.

R: Yes. They were honored to be here, so the whole house was just aglow with a lot of love, and that felt good. Not everyone was with me every second. Steve was with me almost the whole time, but everyone else would rotate. It was perfect, just perfect. So I'm sitting on my bed and they put on this tape and I listened to it and, Oh boy, that . . .

S: This was your affirmation tape.

R: This was the tape where everyone talked to the baby, we chanted, and it had my affirmations on it, and I started hearing those: My mind is God's mind, my body is God's body, and my spirit is God's spirit. I just started crying, and I was crying from joy, but it was a release. I felt so blessed to be having this child. I felt blessed to have Cathy, who was sitting on the bed with me, who I love dearly. We both started crying, and the room just filled with white light. I felt absolute 100 percent unconditional love for myself.

S: Great. How often were your contractions at that point?

R: They were just constant.

S: They were constant?

R: Yes, it was constant energy and it was beautiful. I thought, what a wonderful gift I have given myself to make this tape. Cathy checked me again and I had completely dilated. For a couple of hours there at the end, one side of my cervix had totally dilated, and the other side hadn't caught up yet. Probably I had been lying on one side for quite awhile and dilated unevenly, and so I had an hour-and-a half right there on the bed where I was waiting for the other side to open up. When I was completely dilated, in that last phase, I was really excited. People were getting the tub ready and Steve was taking a shower and scrubbing up with iodine. I had had two enemas during the day; I wanted to be very clean when I was in the tub. So I was completely dilated and everyone was preparing the tub, we had the candles lighted, the videotape was set up, and Peter was ready with two or three cameras. Everyone was very excited when I got in the tub. I had my red-lips plastic pillow in the tub.

S: I saw it this morning. It reminded me of the birth films.

R: I could float on the pillow, hang my arms over the pillow, rest my head on it, lean on it, and it was great. The water was wonderful. It was 100 degrees Fahrenheit. Water to me is calm, it feels great.

S: How had they been heating the water?

R: We used hot tap water and kept it at 100 degrees by watching the thermometer and pouring in a little more warm water if we needed it. The room was also warm and we had a little heater if we needed it. I was ready for the baby to come out. Steve was in the water with me, and it was time to do what they call pushing the baby out. The baby will probably come out whether you push or not, because that's what the contractions—expansions are doing, but you can work with that energy and assist the baby. You should *not* hold your breath when you push a baby out, if you can help it, and definitely not longer than four or five seconds. When women push they tend to hold their breath. But when you hold your breath, the baby's not getting any oxygen. I'd been doing connective breathing most of my labor, and I didn't want to quit breathing for pushing, yet I wanted to help the baby come out. I'd been to about 8 or 10 births before Mela. I'd watched women in the pushing stage, and I had it in my head how you push. There's quite an art to it. You're relaxing your legs, your thighs, your whole pelvic floor, while at the same time you are tensing and tightening your diaphragm and abdominal muscles. The tendency for most people, when they tighten their abdomen and diaphragm is to tighten their legs and their buttocks, and you don't do this. There's a little art to that, and I feel that my body work helped me to master that idea of tightening one muscle and letting another be totally relaxed.

It took me about five or six contractions to master it. One person said to try making a low, gutteral kind of sound with the contraction. I tried that, and it didn't feel right at all. Finally it just clicked in my mind, and I started breathing . . .

S: You got it that the way to have this baby was to breathe it out?

R: Right. So I'm in the tub and everybody is cheering me on. When I really got it about breathing with the contractions, Steve was grinning from ear to ear. There's a photograph we have of him and I've never seen his mouth so wide in my whole life!

S: He was in the tub with you then?

R: Yes. I knew at that point it was only going to be a few minutes. The contraction would come and I would just breathe hard down, down, down, breathe down.

S: How long had you then been in the tub?

R: Oh, about fifteen minutes.

S: So you didn't get in this tub until the last hour?

R: Right. All together, it was 35 minutes from when I got in the tub until the baby came out. You think "Wow, what am I going to do? It can't go upward, it can't go backwards. Finally you know you're assisting the baby because you can feel her head moving down through the vagina. I was on all fours . . . I did pushing like that, squatting on my feet in the tub and holding onto Steve or the sides of the tub. I also did it by being on my knees with my arms and my head resting on my little pillows. When she was about to come out I said I wanted to turn on my back and watch her in the mirror. I had my friends hold the mirror above my head so I could watch her. When a baby is born it's such a beautiful process. The head comes out, you'll see it, then it will go back in, then you'll see the head a little more and it'll go back in. It's like two steps forward, and one step back—it's a little process, a little dance, and I wanted to watch the whole thing.

S: So you had the mirror?

R: Yes. Abby and Arthur and others held it above my head, and I put my legs on the side of the tub with towels underneath them—also, friends held them for me—and I just watched her and relaxed my whole lower body. I could see her head come up; it was very white with the cream-cheesy substance that protects their skin when they're in the womb. I'd watch her little head come out and then go back in, come out and go back in. The contractions at this part of labor are different from the earlier contractions. They're further apart and a little bit slower; it's not quite as intense and there would be little rest periods in between. We monitored her heartbeat underwater with a fetuscope, and her heartbeat was 140 the whole time, really good. She was getting plenty of oxygen, I knew that, so I would just push down and she'd come out a little bit further, a little further, and then you knew that two or three more contractions and she was going to be out.

Mary Michael was very helpful to me with pushing. She's attended a thousand births, and she would just say that's good, that's good, and just rest, because sometimes she didn't want to push, she wanted to relax and let the energy of the baby work on the muscles. If you are pushing but you're not relaxed you'll tear. It's a very delicate process of being with the energy and with your body. Then Mela's head started coming out and everybody said, "It's a girl, don't you think?" I reached down and touched her head and that was a complete circle. She was inside of me, but also outside enough for me to touch her head, and it felt very beautiful. I felt my energy get even more focused.

I didn't want to test it and risk putting too much strain on her, so Steve held her and I just touched her and loved her. We had agreed to surrender to the baby and allow her to tell us psychically when she was ready to come up. I didn't want any emergency around bringing her up or keeping her down, so we just let it be. While she was underwater, a total of 7 minutes, Steve started moving her hands around a little bit. She would swallow water and spit it out, and little clouds of stuff came out of her mouth two or three times. That was pretty intense for some people in the room.

S: I think most people who fear the baby will be drowned are forgetting that the baby is in water the whole nine months, so it's used to that.

R: Right after that she sat up (lifted up her head and upper body underwater), opened her eyes, looked right at me, and it was like she smiled.

S: Wow, under water!

R: It was just like she was saying "Hello! I love you and here I am." I had a gushing of love come out of me towards Mela and said "I want to hold her." The cord had just started dropping a little bit, so we brought her up and I held her out of the water in my arms. I held her face down in case she had any fluids to come out. She didn't. She just started breathing within, I don't know, half a minute.

S: Started breathing?

R: Little breaths out of her nose, just little bitty ones, I could hear them. Then all of a sudden, gasp, there was a great big inhale, and you could hear the breath in her lungs. After that she was breathing fully and freely and connectedly

156

in the way that you would ideally like to see all of your re-birthing clients breathe.

S: Really, how wonderful, every rebirther's dream!

R: And she was just fine. We had a little blanket over her, and the cord kept pulsing for another half hour at least. In dry births cords quit pulsing in 5 to 10 minutes; I feel the cord lasted so long because it was mostly under the water. It didn't just quit pulsing, so Mela had an auxiliary oxygen supply for 45 minutes after she was born. The air in the room was warm, and she had auxiliary oxygen, and she learned to breathe without a trace of any trauma or emergency or difficulty at all. I feel, for her, breath was pleasure.

S: She didn't have any of that choking . . .

R: She didn't sputter, choke, anything.

S: Did you put her to the breast?

R: Not right then. She just breathed and wanted to look at us. Also, she had her eyes closed sometimes, so we cleared the room and were there by ourselves with her. Then I felt it was time to cut the cord, so Cathy came in and we cut the cord and I stood up. When I stood up, the placenta came out and they caught it in a bowl. Steve took Mela in the bedroom, which was warm, while I dried off and put on a robe. I went into the bedroom and he was doing a little jiggling massage with her. He'd take her little arms, her little hands, and gently move them. When I came in she was smiling, lying on the bed, open and relaxed. She was obviously in total bliss, as was Steve. He felt so blessed that he was able to share this touching communication with her for those few minutes. I just looked at her and smiled at her and continued to talk to her as we had while she was born—saying welcome to the world, we're so glad your here, the universe loves and supports you, just every nice thought we could think of. I held her and put her to the breast, and she didn't really want it right away. For the first hour or two after birth she wanted to look at us. We looked and smiled and talked. I felt aeons of ancient remembering when I looked at her; years and years of knowing her was what I was feeling in my body. It was like "Here we are again, and this is so wonderful," and I was acknowledging both of us for being who we were. There was a lot of telepathic communication. Then after about 1 or 2 hours she started sucking, and that's another whole new experience.

The real milk does not come in for 2 or 3 days, so the first liquid they get is a little fluid called colostrum, which has a lot of nutrients and natural antibodies in it. I just sat there and smiled about this nursing relationship. You know, it took several days for her to really master the sucking. She would get it and then the nipple would fall out of her mouth and she'd have to look for it. There was a whole art to that and I realized that probably in the past a lot of women tried to nurse the first few days, and they'd think they didn't have enough milk.

S: They gave up too soon?

R: They gave up too soon. I had those feelings the first few days. I had feelings come up about not enough. Then I said, no, she's fine. She's been living just fine, and those three days where you just have *colustrum*, it's what they need. Just as you don't just come off a very high experience and go eat steaks and potatoes and heavy food, but are gentle with yourself and easy with your body, so I realized that those three days are perfectly harmonious. She doesn't have too much to process, her digestive system is just starting up. She's starting to have bowel movements, she's learning to suck, using her cheek and throat muscles—a lot of learning is going on. So those three days were perfect. I did realize that in the past if women didn't know, or doctors didn't know, they'd think "Oh, no, you can't nurse, not enough milk," and you'd just go along with that. So those first hours after birth I feel, are very, very important in any baby's life and it's important that you're just there.

S: Weren't you glad you weren't removed from here for any reason?

R: We were not separated at all. I walked in the kitchen one time and Steve had her and she knew we were there. She was right in the same bed where she'd been for nine months, you know, right in between her mom and dad, and everything was just perfect. In that first week after birth I feel it's very important that the mother and father *both* be there, that somebody *else* is in the house to clean, cook, run errands, answer the phone, to assist and serve you in any way, so that you are totally free to just be in this new relationship. You know, when you fall in love with someone, it's a whole thing. You go through a process of getting to know each other and being together, allowing your lives to adapt to each other. Well, that's what it's like. You have a baby, a new being, and you're just getting used to that relationship, so I recommend—actually, I recommend that people have assistance for three months.

S: That's a good idea.

R: Well, that's ideal. To be financially independent enough that you don't have to worry about money and you have your needs met for three months at least, and you have people to love and support you. My parents came up the next day (they live about an hour-and-a-half from here) and it was wonderful for Mela to see her grandparents and them to see her. They didn't know the birth was going to be underwater because we decided only in the last few days. They knew it was a possibility, but my mother said "I don't want to know when you're in labor, I just want to know when it's over." Well, my mother is very psychic, and she called that morning while I was in labor. Those first 7 days are a time to nurture and love yourself and be with the baby, so we took her outside and talked to her and just really let her know we were here for her.

S: Great. You and Steve just stayed around the bed with her for the first few days postpartum, and others took care of everything else. Did you have any problems with bleeding or anything?

R: I had no problems with bleeding. I had no infections, I had no tears, I had nothing. I felt very good. I was a little tired. Preparing for a birth, is like preparing for a major athletic event. It's like the Superbowl. It's not something that women are doing everyday, it's something that you may do one, two or three times in your life, and you prepare for it accordingly.

After the birth I felt extremely high and full of energy and love, and I also felt like resting my body. I'd done enough. I got massages and Steve was very wonderful, supportive and loving. I was learning how to hold the baby comfortably while I nursed. I was learning a lot of things: how to sit, how to hold her, how to nurse her lying down. When my milk came in, Mela got high on milk. Here was her first milk, she had plenty of it coming out both breasts, and she was just in bliss. She would look up at me and send me this message that this milk is wonderful. If you've ever tasted breast milk it is very sweet, much sweeter than chocolate fudge sundaes or anything I have ever tasted. It is very sweet and just got to be good. I realized that nursing was one of her first experiences on the outside of abundance. I would let her know when she nursed that there was always more than enough for her. There's an abundance of milk and an abundance of love, and there would always be an abundance of everything for her.

S: That makes me wish I had been breastfed.

R: I'd read a couple of books on nursing and I found that they used to schedule babies, even on nursing; they'd say you

160

can nurse between this hour and this hour, but not here, or you can only nurse this way, and they had a schedule for feedings, so I didn't do that. I just nursed her whenever she wanted it. So in those first few weeks she nursed (I think this is pretty ordinary) every 45 minutes to an hour-and-a-half. Newborns can't hold all that much you know, and so they nurse frequently. I guess the longest she slept in those first weeks was three, maybe four hours at a time, and so I like to tell parents to handle their sleep cases and handle thoughts about sleep and rest and all that.

S: Can you give an example of an affirmation you did?

R: One of my affirmations was "I'm rested whether I sleep or not." Also the day after I had her I lay down beside her and she rebirthed me. I said "Okay, I am here to serve you and I totally surrender to you," and I lay next to her and did connective breathing. I just kept giving up and giving up and I said "I have nothing better to do than to totally serve you. That's it." I said "My mind might come up with, oh, you think you have to do this, you have to do that, no, I have nothing better to do in my life right now than to love you and serve you and I surrender to you." God, that was wonderful.

S: And she got it, too. You knew she knew what you were saying.

R: Right. About sleep, your mind will say "I should sleep seven hours, I should do this, I should do that," so in the past parents have had to control their children in order to live up to their expectations about sleep and rest and other things. I said no, what I'm doing with this baby is surrendering to her, and that's it, and if that means we do nursing every 45 minutes, great, if we nurse every 5 hours, great, whatever we do is fine with me. So that's what I did, and if I sometimes felt irritable, it would never be her fault. If I was irritable I'd look at myself, and usually I was having some feelings about my not getting all the nurturing I thought I should have had when *I* was a baby. Then I would call Arthur, or Steve, and I'd have them give me a massage. Or I would lie down and rebirth myself with Mela so I would not blame her, because it has nothing to do with her. It has to do with me. I would handle whatever thoughts or feelings I had, and I had some stuff going about not getting what I wanted when I wanted it as a baby. It was wonderful to realize that it wasn't her fault and I could use this as an opportunity to heal myself.

I tell parents that they don't need sleep to feel rested, but they do need love and support, and they do need to take care of themselves. Sometimes women will have a baby and allow people to help them for three days, then after that they try to be the supermoms; they're out there sweeping the porch and cleaning the house, that's ridiculous. It's important that you let people love you. Serving a new mother or a pregnant woman is one of the highest gifts anybody can give, so I always encourage parents and pregnant women to allow people to serve them. It's an honor.

S: That's good. What else have you learned about yourself since her birth?

R: Well, I was wondering why Mela's birth took 17 hours when I thought it would be 8 to 12. I had a very interesting realization at the Loving Relationships Training in Houston in February after she was born in November. Mallie Mandell, the trainer, said "I know this client who's an incubator baby, and I realized that incubator babies have two births, one from the womb and one from their incubator." All of a sudden my knees turned to jelly and my legs started shaking—I could hardly stand up. I was in an incubator for five days or so after my birth because I weighed only 4 pounds. The incubator was in my mother's room. I was not separated from her, but I remember that other people decided I was ready to be out of my incubator, though psychically *I* never did that, so I had this mental invisible shield around me all the time of *not quite being ready yet*. In Mela's birth what I created was: I wasn't quite ready, I needed just a little more time to be fully ready, and I had integrated my thought to the extent that if I had extra time I could be ready. When I had this realization that February, I realized that I am ready now, I don't have to have extra time any more. I might have it, but I don't need it. When I had the realization that I'm ready now, that it is safe for me to be outside my protective incubator, I had fear rush through my body for about an hour. I could hardly walk, I could hardly be in the elevator going up to my room, and I had to breathe all of that out. I realize that, emotionally and psychically, I'd always kept this little shield around me because I needed to have a mental incubator.

S: That's interesting. So you got delivered from the incubator postpartum?

R: Right. I realized that if I were to give birth again it would definitely be different, because I don't have that thought anymore about needing extra time in order to be ready. If I had another baby it would take less time.

S: You had a career. How did you deal with that?

R: Well, after I had Mela I realized that I had set up in my mind that it was okay to be fully a mother for a few months, and then after I had all these "shoulds." I should do this much work, I should start rebirthing people, I should start doing my career. I had some stress with that because I kept feeling pulled not to do much work. I wanted only to be there with Mela, and I went through some sadness. I had thoughts that being a mother wasn't as good as my other career, and that if I just devoted myself fully to being a mother till I felt like doing something else I might lose out, you know, people would forget me and I wouldn't . . .

S: You wouldn't keep up with your career?

R: Right. I had all these thoughts come up that I think are common, people have had them a lot. I wasn't allowing myself to realize that being a mother is as good a career as any of my other careers.

S: So you finally realized that and then it worked?

R: I can't remember exactly when or how, but something happened. Perhaps somebody said "Look, being a mother is a wonderful career," and I just got it. Being a mother *is* enough, and it's a wonderful career. Not only that, I realized that being a mother could only enhance any other careers that I would choose—because of the process of healing myself by being a mother. Babies will bring up anything in the parents that they have not resolved about their own infancy, or childhood, so for me to be with Mela from the beginning all the way through heals me at whatever level was incomplete with me in my infancy. There were some days in those first few months that you couldn't tell who was the baby, Mela or me!

S: You felt like a baby?

R: I felt just like a baby. I'd want to suck on nipples and bottles, and I'd just want to lie in bed, so I let myself do that. I would rewrite the scripts that came up in my mind about infancy and motherhood; I realized that I was in a very exclusive, wonderful training being a mother with Mela, and then I should just consider it an investment in my total life and my total well-being. Any career that I chose or any projects I chose to do would only be enhanced by my being a mother.

S: She does travel with you, right?

R: She does everything.

S: That works all right?

R: Yes. Actually, my career is in total harmony with all of this because I'm a rebirther. Everything I do is definitely enhanced by being Mela's mother, and Mela and I have rebirthed may people together, people have been very healed by her presence. She's been to large trainings and she generally loves it. When the time comes that she would rather be doing something else, she will have that. If I'm leading a training, she can have someone to take her out to play. I feel that everything can be worked out for her highest good and my highest good. Basically, I'm not into forcing her to be away from me or Steve, and that's not what she wants, so this first year (she's 11 months now) has been a process of integrating her into our lives. Of course, most of our friends totally welcome her into their lives, and I think it's important to remember that babies are not really babies.

S: That's a good point. They're adults in small bodies.

R: They're equally as divine and intelligent as we are.

S: I think people forget they've had many reincarnations and thus arrive with Infinite Intelligence. They should be reminded of that.

R: Right. We're just playing this baby-mama game, but it's not what the Absolute Truth is about. The Absolute Truth is that Mela and I are equals, and this is a convenient way for her to master her body and develop herself, and for us to be in a relationship. I mean, I love playing mama and everything else, but I do know the truth. The truth is that I look at her and she looks right back at me and we both know everything. It's so important for parents to remember that children are not really children.

S: You treat her as you would an adult, with respect, don't you?

R: Yes.

S: How has this affected your finances, and your marriage, and so on? Has having a baby been expensive, has it been a strain on you financially?

R: Well, no. Having a baby probably cost us about $1,000.

S: That's pretty cheap.

R: Yes, and you know, we would be more prepared financially for another one. With Mela we had 3 or 4 weeks of living without needing to work for money, and I would now choose to extend that to three months. Steve took over earning most of our money the first few months, so I didn't need to worry about that. My affirmation was that having a baby is profitable, and I have found that to be true.

S: You started saying that affirmation early in pregnancy?

R: Right. I got that even before we got pregnant. Before we conceived, someone said to me "Babies cost money" and I decided that's not the thought we want. I love the thought "Having a baby increases your prosperity." That thought could just as easily be true as the one that having a baby decreases your income.

S: Can you give me some examples of how it can be true?

R: Well for one thing, every time you open your heart and let more love into your life, that's going to transfer to all levels of your life. When you have a baby, you open yourself to receive a lot more love. I feel that this willingness to receive and expand yourself transfers to your life, to your financial life as well. People tend to get raises and to find new ways of making money because increasing love in their life expands everything. We made more money last year than ever before, and I worked less.

S: That's good. Do you have any other advice to parents about careers and finances?

R: No, but I encourage parents to honor the career of motherhood and to let mothers know that being a mother is just as good as being a rebirther or an artist or a plumber or anything else. I also think that acknowledgment of motherhood from friends and family is very important. You know, the first few months my friends acknowledged me a lot. When I leave trainings people will come up and say "You're a great trainer, I got so much out of the seminar," so I had people talk to me about motherhood just as they would talk to me about being a rebirther. "You are such a great mother, and I get so much out of being around you and Mela and seeing how you relate to her," and I started getting it. I started feeling that acknowledgment. Of course, now I work with pregnant women and couples and families and I'm able to share very intimately what I learned with others, so I do get a lot of acknowledgment for being a mother.

S: So you feel really happy you did the birth the way you did. Would you do anything different?

R: Let's see, I would have champagne after the birth. After Mela's birth I had wine. I hardly drank alcohol during my pregnancy. It just didn't taste good to me. After she was born somebody brought me a glass of red wine and it tasted like the most divine substance in the universe. But champagne is one of my favorites, so I think the next time I would have champagne.

S: You'd do it just the same except you'd have champagne?

R: Well, I'd do it in the water again. I might make a few little technical improvements in the tub and in the room. The tub could be about six inches wider and have a very soft, molded kind of chair to recline in. I would have padding around the sides of the tub so the people who leaned on the edges would be comfortable and if I put my legs up there they would be comfortable. I would be even more *present* than ever before, because that's how I am now. I feel it would be even easier now, because since we've been going around the country giving lectures I know five or six couples who have done underwater births and more who are planning them. Just as with rebirthing, after more and more people do it the psychic space of safety increases and makes it even easier. You know, when we had Mela we only knew of two other underwater births in this country.

S: You were pioneers.

R: So I feel there would be even more safety within the people who attended the birth and within us. Even though I felt safety in Mela's birth, it would be even greater now.

S: She certainly has been healthy. She's a picture of health and total harmony to me, so she must be happy to have been born underwater. You haven't had any problems with her health, have you?

R: No, she's totally healthy, weighs 20 pounds now. She likes being in the water, she's had swimming classes.

S: When did you start having her swim?

R: She had swimming lessons this past July, at 8 months. I tell people that Mela does not have the shadow of fear or trauma about her that I've seen babies have. She knows she's loved and she gives a lot to people. She's very alert and inquisitive and aware and happy.

S: I've always seen her happy, totally beautiful, harmonized, and easy to be with. I think she's a miracle. Is there anything else you'd like to say about pregnancy and birth before we wrap it up?

R: I feel that women should do things with their bodies that they feel nurture them. I feel that it is valuable to have a good naturopathic or homeopathic physician or a good chiropractor, a good M.D.—people about whom you feel good to serve you at the physical level. It would be good to have your muscles balanced, your spine balanced, your cranium balanced; it's good to have your body in harmony with your thoughts and to do what supports that for you.

S: Any other thoughts?

R: One of the first thoughts I had after Mela's birth was that the best gift you can give your child is a clear consciousness.

S: That seems like a good idea.

R: I mean, that's ultimately even better than the water or the Leboyer method or any technique you might choose. When I was born I just bonded to my parents entire consciousness; I just loved them totally and I loved their thoughts, and of course one of the thoughts they had was that death was inevitable. You know, they believed that you have to live and die in the physical body, and when I had a baby in 1968 I also had that thought, so while I was giving birth I had lots of thoughts of death. When I had Mela I had thoughts of life; I know that we are at choice over our bodies and our lives, that if we choose to die then it's our choice. I realized that through me Mela was bonding to immortality rather than to mortal consciousness. I feel the absolute best gift you can give your child is a consciousness that knows that life is eternal, that the universe is abundant, that life is not based on scarcity and death but on abundance and love and mastery and choice, and a being that comes into the world and bonds to that consciousness has already got a zillion-year start on what I had.

S: I like the way you said that. I have had a great time interviewing you about this birth. I guess everybody's question would be "Well, what if it doesn't work like that? It sounds ideal, but what if mine isn't that ideal? What do I do, and what does it mean?"

R: That's a question I've thought about a lot, because since Mela's birth I've been to four or five more births, and altogether I've been to probably a dozen births, and frequently something happens that isn't as you planned. You might plan an underwater birth and then end up having to go to the hospital, or you might plan to have your birth at home and something else happens. So what do you do when it doesn't turn out as you planned? One of the first things that comes up with people is that they want to blame. I tell people just to accept the perfection of the kind of birth you had, whether it's at home or in the hospital, whether the baby comes out in the normal way or some other, whether there's some kind of complication. There is a lesson in this and a perfection in it. Perhaps some thoughts need to come to your attention by this experience, or the being coming through you needs to manifest its thoughts by having some kind of complication come up. Ultimately, there's no one to blame. Blame is off the track. What you can do is to love yourself and surrender to the perfection of what happened. When Mela's birth was several hours longer than I planned, I could have said "Oh, you must be a stupid, bad person because you couldn't create a birth in the number of hours you wanted," but the truth is that I now clearly see why that happened, and that it was appropriate. She probably enjoyed having that extra time, so it was appropriate.

S: And it was related to your birth.

R: It helped me clear a birth thought of mine. We're always clearing, and we're always opening and expanding, so I tell people to be flexible, do you know, be flexible with yourself. You can say I want this ideal birth with a tub and water, and

I want the baby's head to come out first, but be willing to be flexible, because you're going to get something better for you and the baby and everyone, and so-called complications can be better for you than what you might have planned.

S: There might be some very powerful lesson that one needs to get. Well, let's talk a little bit about spirituality and pregnancy. You are obviously a lot more spiritual than you were when you were pregnant the first time. How do you feel that affected you?

R: This time?

S: Did you feel it made a difference?

R: Well, that's the key to the ideal birth. If you have the thought that you are separate from God, or that God is separate from you, and you're in labor, it can be frightening. Birth is a process of trust and surrender, and if you're thinking you're separate from God—and therefore you have to be in control and handle everything in order to be safe—well, you don't have time to do that and have a baby. So I feel that getting straight and clear on your relationship with God (or Divinity, or Infinite Being, or whatever you want to call that Principle) is of utmost importance in preparing for childbirth and in giving birth. We are all connected, but we're not just what we see and feel and touch; we're connected at a very spiritual level, so I always encourage people to be clear in their relationship with God. God is not out there to hurt us or to do us any harm. God loves us unconditionally every moment, and God's not there making us wrong if our birth turns out differently than we planned. God is saying yes to whatever's going on with us, and we can look at the results we get in our birth and learn from them. There's a huge margin of safety in the universe, and we are safe. We're safe in hospitals, in our homes, in automobiles. Ultimately birth is a safe, natural, family experience wherever it is.

S: One of the things that I feel is different about your pregnancy from a lot that I assisted as a prenatal nurse is that you were clear on the truth that THOUGHT IS CREATIVE and that you create your own reality with your thoughts. So you were always aware how your thoughts were affecting your marriage and your baby. I think that is one of the key things, and the result is to have such a positive, healthy, beautiful, perfect baby. It was a perfect birth. That's it! It was the ideal birth.

Interview with Steven Star, Mela's Father

S: I would like to hear your theory of underwater birth and why you think it's important. As one of the first fathers in America to have tried it, please say anything you want about it.

ST: To give you a little background, I originally had the idea of underwater birth after experiencing what they call underwater rebirthing almost seven years ago. After I'd attended a number of underwater rebirthings, and had experienced the exquisite pleasure that I got from rebirthing myself in water, it just came to me. I was thinking how much I'd enjoyed breathing under water, how supportive and pleasurable it felt to my body, and how wonderfully safe the environment felt to me. So it struck me that, my God, it would be incredible if a baby could just come out of the womb underwater and get to hang out there and experience this extended womb.

S: I like that phrase, *extended womb.*

ST: You know, it hit me, it really hit. It was a powerful image and feeling I had when I was visualizing this.

172

S: This was after you heard about the Russian Method?

ST: No, no, no. This was about seven years ago.

S: You hadn't even heard about the Russian Method?

ST: No, never. It came from my own experience of underwater rebirthing, and of course the whole theory behind Dr. Leboyer's method. He really caught my imagination when he said to put yourself in the baby's position and then think of all the ways that you could create that baby's coming into the world in the most loving and gradual way possible, so it would be able to experience each nuance very gradually, so it would have time to integrate its experience. That's how Leboyer created his technique. Having seen so many babies, he visualized himself as the baby and then used his imagination to think of every way he could introduce each nuance of sensory input as gradually and lovingly as possible. I was very excited about this idea. There was an urge in my heart to find some medical people and try to jazz them up with this idea so that they'd experiment with it, but I had no strong motivation at that time to do it. It wasn't until my wife and I were considering conceiving that we first started hearing about underwater birth in Russia. We first read about it in the *National Enquirer,* and then we started seeing articles once in a while. They never gave any technical information, but seemed to convey that birthing babies underwater and allowing them to be in water uninterrupted for a full 24 hours—or as much as possible for the first day—was extremely beneficial.

The Russians said it would create beings with a tremendous sense of balance, who would be great athletes. It would give newborns the immediate freedom to do all types of rhythmic movements. They also felt it would create human beings who were able to adapt to the weightlessness of outer space and it would increase intelligence. So it was three things: better sense of balance, a better sense of rhythm and freedom of motion (very agile), and easier adaptation to a different gravity system associated with increased intelligence. A book that was very influential in my enthusiasm and understanding of the possibilities of underwater birth was *The Magical Child* by Joseph Chilton Pearce (New York: Bantam, 1980).

S: What made you think of underwater birth after reading that book?

ST: Well, in his book Pearce talks about the stress of the baby's coming down the birth canal. That stress triggers the flow of adrenaline and all sorts of hormones into the bloodstream. Those hormones and adrenaline are used to build neuropathways to the brain. There is a tremendous leap in consciousness that takes place then. They say the first day is critical for what they call a rapid brain growth spurt.

S: That's what Pearce is talking about in that book.

ST: Yes, he has compiled all this information for an overview of the natural progression of innate intelligence.

S: How did reading that book relate to underwater birth?

ST: Getting back to the first 24 hours—the first rapid brain growth spurt—Pearce says that stillness is the enemy of the newborn, because stillness drastically cuts down the learning process. So I thought maybe spending the first 24 hours in water would provide the perfect environment for tremendous, uninterrupted learning. It would exponentially expand the possibilities over the traditional method where most infants are immediately washed off, clothed, wrapped in blankets, and left in stillness for long periods of time.

S: So after reading that book you wanted even more to do this?

ST: Oh yeah, it totally excited me. Pearce also talks about another interesting thing that made sense of underwater birth. He talks about going from the known (life in the womb) to the unknown (life outside the womb), and that there's a natural cycle in learning situations where you go from the known to the unknown. When you get stressed out or afraid of the unknown you need to come back to the known where you're safe and can relax. Leaving the child with the mother gives it a reference point in the known, which is its mother. Separation from the mother disrupts the known and puts the baby into total stress. So I thought, with underwater birth, the baby comes out in an environment that is totally known because it's liquid. Immediately the baby will be able to relax from the stress of coming through the birth canal, feel completely supported and familiar and safe, and integrate that passage before it has to learn to breathe. Once it has relaxed and has integrated that experience, then it's completely open and aware and ready to take on gravity and the drying of the skin and a different sense of touch. There is a tremendous adjustment to sound and light and, most important, breathing.

S: It's a good theory. Was that your experience?

ST: First there's one more thing I want to cover about the value of underwater birth. This theory has only been proven over two births that I know of personally, by people who had enough courage and intuitive certainty that it's safe to leave babies underwater for longer than a couple of seconds. The most important information passed on to me by Patrick and Jia was that babies breathe *in utero*—well, they don't really breathe but they pull the water in and out of the breathing mechanism. Perhaps they do this to exercise those muscles.

S: They've actually recorded this in the fetus?

ST: Yes. It was done with intrauterine photography. Patrick and Jia told us that once their baby had been born into the water, they were holding him there for a time (I don't know if it was five minutes or ten minutes) but it looked as if the baby was making respiratory attempts in the water. When it started happening with our baby Mela, we were prepared for it. They said to relax, it's natural, there's nothing harmful happening and you can give up your concern.

S: The baby's still connected through the cord.

ST: It's getting all the necessary oxygen through the cord.

S: So these sucking movements don't hurt anything.

ST: They don't hurt anything, but it is my theory that the value of that natural reflex is to rinse out the mucous that's in babies' breathing mechanisms when they come out of the womb. I've been present at any number of births, dry births, and when a baby comes out and has to breath immediately, that mucous gets kind of pulled towards their lungs and then as they exhale it has a tendency to come back out. It doesn't really get expelled easily, so on the next breath it gets pulled back down towards their breathing mechanism.

Some babies have a real problem. The birth attendants either have to suction them or turn them upside down and put their fingers in there and try to pull some of that stuff out.

S: Did you see something coming out of your daughter's mouth?

ST: Well, yeah, when she was underwater and she started making those respiratory attempts we saw a kind of opaque pinkish cloud coming out of her mouth and nose each time her chest would heave, and it looked like she was making respiratory attempts.

S: Did that make you nervous at all?

ST: Well, it didn't make me too nervous because our friends warned us about it ahead of time. It is kind of dramatic and, when you actually see it, it's just strange.

S: So you just let her do it?

ST: Yes.

S: Did she stop doing it finally?

ST: Well, she did about six of those things, then she stopped and was just still, as if she was in a deep meditation. About a minute after that, as I was holding her in my hands, she sat up at the waist and I had to kind of drop her towards the bottom of the tub or her head would have come clear out of the water, and she sat just right up, almost at a 90-degree angle, and looked at Rima.

S: Was this by herself?

ST: Yes. A baby would never be able to do that in gravity, but in water she was able to do that—it just seemed effortless for her. I couldn't see her because she had her back to me, but Rima said it was as if, in her eyes and in the expression on her face, she were saying "Hi, mom, I love you," and Rima had this big wave of love go out for her. Then Mela lay back down into my hands and went into what seemed to be this meditation.

S: She'd just sent out signs.

ST: Yes, then she lay down again. Rima was lying back in the tub and she didn't want to sit up and sort of grab for her, because she didn't know whether this would cause any stress on the unbilical cord or the placenta, so she hadn't really made real contact with her other than psychically and emotionally. A minute later Rima said "I want to hold her." Of course I was interested in having her be in that underwater state for as long as possible, or as long as it seemed right. I said "Well, Rima, it's been about 8 minutes."

S: So she actually stayed underwater for 8 minutes? That's a long time. Were you hoping she'd stay a little longer?

ST: No, I was willing for it to unfold the way it was supposed to. I reached up to feel the umbilical cord, because the umbilical cord is the lifeline. If there were any change in that umbilical cord I wanted to know about it, because that would be a sign that there was a need to bring her up for some reason. I felt the cord and noticed that it had dropped about 10 to 15 percent in pressure from when she first came out. I knew Mela was totally relaxed and had integrated that passage, and so the drop in the umbilical cord plus Rima's wanting to hold her made it seem an appropriate time to bring her up. So we brought her up and I gave her to Rima.

Rima laid her face down to her breast and she slumped down into the water with Mela's belly submerged and the cord completely submerged. (Air contact shuts down the umbilical cord. It's air contact with the cord and the contractions after birth that start to separate the placenta from the uterine wall, and we wanted to keep the cord pulsing as long as possible.) When we brought Mela up, she tilted her head down and a little bit of liquid drained out of her; I don't know whether it was just water draining off of her face or whether water came out of her mouth or her breathing mechanism. She just lay there with the cord still pulsing very well. There was still a lot of life support coming through there. She was so relaxed and there was no rush, no real need, to begin lung breathing, so she lay there for about 45 seconds. Then Rima said, "I think she's breathing," so I put my ear right next to her head and I could hear she was just very gently trying to pull a breath. She was making these very gentle attempts to breathe. They were kind of connected, but they were very shallow and very light.

It was just about that time that we all figured that she was actually trying to breathe. Then you could hear one breath. It just went "Hoooo" all the way, and her lungs inflated. It wasn't like this mad gasp for oxygen, it was just gradual, there was no rush or panic to it. She was just playing around with it, kind of feathering it open is what she was doing. Then after that first breath filled her lungs, with hardly any faltering at all, she went right into connected, relaxed rhythm. She would cycle a little bit, as in rebirthing, cycle in and out of different rhythms. But it was without any of that gurgling that you often hear with newborns when they first learn to breathe. I think we'll find in future research—and this proved out in our birth and the birth before—that those seeming respiratory attempts actually rinse the breathing mechanism of that mucous or fluid. A lot of babies who don't really get it out of their lungs have a real tough time learning to breathe. In my estimation this could eventually lead to emphysema and asthma and all sorts of breathing disorders.

S: It seems that, since Mela had time to work that out, her first breath was totally pure.

ST: Yes, she rinsed all that out, it was clean and clear, and that's why she was able immediately to go into connected, relaxed breathing without faltering. At that point I was sitting there in awe, really enjoying looking at my wife and my baby. The peace that came over me was profound. Just seeing my baby was a real miracle. By the way, the midwives had birthed over a thousand babies, and they said that Mela had the most vernix on her skin that they had ever seen on a baby. I think that's very healthy. You know, vernix looks kind of like cream cheese—it's a greasy, waxy substance that covers the skin of newborn babies. I think great physical condition and good nutrition had something to do with the baby's having a lot of vernix on her skin. That vernix is kind of food for the skin. Anyhow, the baby was lying on Rima's chest, still attached to the umbilical cord and breathing on its own. I began to make contact with her again. At first I just laid my hands on her—I didn't even move them—I just laid one hand on her forehead and the other on her little arms and hands, and just rested them there.

S: Movement could have been too much.

ST: Yes, just too much. So I rested them there until I made psychic and emotional contact with her and I felt our awarenesses were connected. Then I very slowly started, just with my thumb, massaging some of the vernix that was on her forehead. Then I moved onto her cheeks, just with my thumb, very slowly and lovingly. This was probably ten or fifteen minutes after she was born. There were a lot of people in the room, and the energy had been quiet and very focused up until then. Well, the exciting part was over and people's focus started to wane a little and they started moving around, going in and out of the doors. Someone accidentally kicked the tub and someone else dropped something off the table. At that, Mela started fussing. She was not actually crying, just letting them know "Hey, quiet it down around here and focus it again, or whatever." She was just going kind of "Unnh, unnh," you know. So I said "I don't care what you're doing; everybody just drop whatever you're doing and leave." Everybody was real nice about it. They filed out the door. And then we had about 10 minutes or 15 minutes of uninterrupted time just to be with each other.

S: Right in this room, right?

ST: In this room. It was wonderful to have that space all to ourselves and make contact together with the baby. We had been making contact individually, but not like the shared contact that happened after everybody left. It was as if Rima and I and the baby all met together and shared a very intimate space with a very lovely connection and bonding.

After about ten minutes one of the midwives peeked in and said "Hey, do you think you want to cut the cord yet?" And I said "Yeah, come back in." It had been 30 or 40 minutes since she had come out of the water and started her breathing. Although the cord was still pulsing every once in a while, it was really slow. So the midwife gave me the umbilical clamp and I clamped it off about an inch from her belly. Then the midwife fastened a hemostat about an inch beyond the clamp and gave me the scissors. And I got to cut my daughter's umbilical cord.

S: How did that feel?

ST: It was kind of anticlimatic. But it was an honor to do that; it was a nice ritual. Then the midwife picked the baby up, with the little kind of damp blanket that was on her, and handed her to me. When she started assisting Rima to get out of the tub, the placenta delivered. So the midwife and Rima were busy delivering the placenta and then stimulating the uterus to contract to stop any bleeding that might happen after delivering the placenta. While they were busy with that, I took the baby and sat down in a chair and started making contact with her again. It was just tremendous. She was smiling at me, you know, and there was so much love in her eyes. She would divert her eyes, and then she would come back and catch my eyes again, and there was so much incredible love it was almost amazing.

In bonding with my daughter I was in awe of her awareness, her ability to communicate her love, and a sense of playfulness and personality already in her eyes. She was smiling at me and everything!

S: And they used to say babies don't smile for hours or days! She was smiling immediately.

ST: Oh, immediately. Meanwhile, Rima was taking a shower and getting ready to get into bed and be with the baby, allow her to nurse, and so on. So I went into the bedroom— which was preheated so we didn't have to put clothing or blankets on the baby—and I continued gently massaging the vernix into every little crack and crevice of her body.

And I started doing this technique, which is called a Trager Massage, that I had experienced myself. It is a technique where they kind of jiggle and rock and pat you. It was so pleasurable to me, and I understand why people jiggle and pat and shake and rock babies.

S: Where did you learn this kind of massage?

ST: Well, Dr. Trager's from Hawaii. This is getting to be a popular form of massage.

S: Oh, yes. You did that?

ST: Well, I haven't formally learned Trager Massage, but I had quite a few of them so I knew the principle. So, after I had massaged the vernix into her skin, I began very gently to jiggle and shake her limbs and rock her pelvis, because I knew from Pearce's book that stillness is the enemy of the newborn and that movement creates learning. What I wanted to do was stimulate her autonomic nervous system. I also wanted to give her pleasure in her body—to give her the experience that being in the world as a total organism is a complete pleasure. That it is even more pleasurable than being in the womb. I wanted to convey that it is absolutely safe—and a total sensual treat. I wasn't forcing this on her. I constantly honored her own will to move. If she would want to move her arm this way or that, or move her leg, or didn't like what I was doing, I would always go with her movement—what she wanted to do. As she would relax, I would give it direction and go back into the jiggling, rocking and shaking. So it was a dance that we did together for about 10 minutes.

S: Were you on the bed all this time?

ST: Yes. Rima came in the last 3 or 4 minutes of that and we were actually playing. Mela was becoming so safe and receiving so much pleasure that we were actually playing. You know, most people have the idea that newborns are very delicate and you have to treat them very carefully. Although I was treating her with respect and gentleness, we were playing—we were actually doing a little game together. Then, when we stopped, and left her in stillness, she was in such a state of relaxation and pleasure in her body that she felt completely safe to have her arms and legs fully extended. Most babies are in kind of perpetual motion—but after that massage, Mela's arms and legs stayed completely extended and what I call a bliss smile came over her face that lasted for about 10 minutes. This was not a smile that came and went, but a continuous smile for almost 10 minutes. For me, giving my daughter that gift of experiencing her body and life as total bliss, was a completion of my own birth and the way I wanted it to be for me. I was coming from my own experience of rebirthing. Remembering how it was for me at birth, I wanted to do everything I could possibly think of to make it completely different for my daughter. And it was like a completion of that for me. Giving her that massage and experiencing her bliss, and the safety she felt in her body—that was the highlight of the birth for me.

S: That is a beautiful story. Do you feel ready to talk about your feelings during the pregnancy and the preparation for underwater birth?

ST: Well, from my original idea of it, then having it validated by experience in Russia, then reading Leboyer's books and Pearce's *Magical Child*, there was never any doubt in my mind that I wanted to do it underwater. But my wife—you heard about her experience of losing a baby in water and all of her feelings around that—although in my heart that was the only alternative that excited me, I was willing to surrender to her fear. And was hoping that it would be clear by the time we were ready to deliver.

S: It's interesting how Mela seemed to wait to be born until you got the tub painted. It's as if she really wanted this.

ST: Yes, that was my feeling. Once Rima became certain that she really wanted to do it, and it was safe, and she was supposed to do it that way, Mela started to come. All through the pregnancy I couldn't really get excited about the birth—the delivery and the way we were going to do it—because that wasn't what was in my heart. But when Rima said "I'm absolutely certain that I want to do it underwater. How can we do it?" then it really didn't take me long at all to figure out how to do it. This was my dream the whole pregnancy. And when she said she was certain, boy! I was so excited about this birth I could hardly believe it.

S: How did you know what solution to fill the trough with? Tell me what solutions the Russians used. I'm not clear on this.

ST: I don't know what the Russians use, but our friends in San Diego researched the percentage of salt that needs to be in water to match the salinity of amniotic fluid or tears. They said it was 8 pounds for every 100 gallons of water. Eight pounds of salt—not sea salt, but processed salt, because it is the cleanest. There was nothing there but salt that had been cleaned and processed.

S: Regular table salt?

ST: Well, we went to the grocery story and bought it. But I personally don't think that the salinity of the water is of great importance, because I know of babies being born in just plain tap water with nothing in it.

S: In the hot springs too?

ST: And babies born in hot springs. Babies being born in water that didn't have that much salt in it, but had some salt in it—and they always seem to come out fine.

S: How much salt would you have for this tank?

ST: This is a 250-gallon trough, and we had close to 200 gallons of water in there. So we had just under 16 pounds of salt.

S: Sixteen pounds. That seems like a lot.

ST: It seemed like a lot to us too. We might not have put quite as much as 16 pounds in there.

S: Did you taste it?

ST: When you taste it, it doesn't taste overly salty.

S: Did you have a hose from your bathtub into here?

ST: No, we took 5-gallon plastic buckets from the bathtub to the birthing tub and made a little bucket brigade. We filled the tub just about as fast as you could fill your bathtub. It took about three bathtubs full of water. We have a fairly fast-recovery hot-water heater. I was used to working with these particular types of tanks because I've done a lot of wet rebirthing in them. So I know approximately how long it takes to fill, and how long it's going to take my hot-water heater to recover, and what it takes to maintain a constant temperature. We were shooting for 100°—anywhere between 101 and 98 degrees is the range you would want. We thought right around 100 would be optimal. That was pretty easy to maintain. It takes a good hour for a tub like that to drop a degree or so, and that degree can be gained by dumping just one bucket of hot water into the tub.

S: It seems you felt real certainty about this water process the whole time. Were there any feelings that you had to clear about it?

ST: No, I felt pretty certain about the safety of the whole thing. Although it was all theory I trusted my intuitive knowing.

S: Rima said that during the pregnancy you really were pregnant yourself, and she thought that was great because you had such a feeling of participating. Do you want to talk about that?

ST: Well, yeah, I'd kinda like to talk about all that. A friend of ours, Jack Szumel, who's a certified rebirther, came here and did a seminar called "Handling Your Birth Urge." One of the processes he did in that little seminar was to make a list of all the different kinds of traits you would want in your baby. Then make a list of all the physical traits you'd want it to have from you and all the physical traits you'd want it to have from its mother, or your parents, or her parents. That was really wonderful. It was a real interesting process to do: to think about the best qualities of my physical being and the best qualities of my wife's physical being, and wanting the baby to take the best from both gene pools.

S: How long before you decided to conceive was this?

ST: Oh, we were already pregnant then. I made that list in my head and then I totally gave it up to God. I said "I'd like to have this or something better, God, and it's in your hands. You know the best thing to do."

S: Was that the first time you experienced really getting into the pregnancy? Were you aware of much?

ST: You hear stories of men having morning sickness and going through various emotional states. I didn't have any morning sickness, and I didn't want any, but what I did experience while being pregnant was that our relationship went through some real rollercoasters. And my theory about that whole rollercoaster of emotions in our relationship—is that a baby is a tremendous amount of love, a tremendous condensed package of love, and that amount of love coming into our relationship brought up everything that was suppressed. So it was like a nine-month rebirth; it was a gradual nine-month rebirthing process. There were some stormy times in there, but the last two or three months we started coming really close together. All of that stuff had been cleared out, and we became closer and more connected, and I felt that it was a preparation for this increased amount of love in our lives. So I would suggest that anybody who is pregnant use all the fantastic techniques that are around for clearing yourselves.

S: Can you talk a little about sex and pregnancy?

ST: I'm glad you asked. I never feared that I was going to hurt my daughter, or that she was going to die during our pregnancy. We were going along having fairly wonderful sex and fairly frequently—every week, some sex—and the baby continued to grow and grow. At first there's not much show and you don't feel the baby kicking. Then it got to a point where the baby was really getting out there—I forget what month it was, I'm sure it was six months or more—and one night when we were having sex it just hit me—it never even dawned on me before—that I was having sex with another person too.

S: Making love to two people.

ST: All of a sudden I'm making love with three people, and in my mind it was "Okay, now, how do you feel making love to your wife and making love to your son." I would be making love with my son, if it was a son. And it really boggled my mind.

S: So if it were a boy, it would be "Here I am making love to another male."

ST: Yes. It didn't even dawn on me until this one night when I could feel the baby kicking around in there. And then I thought "Well, if this is a daughter, you're making love to your daughter." This is incest, right? And I knew that my thoughts were affecting my baby *in utero*.

S: Prenatal psychology, they call it now.

ST: I was enlightened about this. So I immediately started searching in my mind to justify this and to find my highest thought about what was happening. Basically I concluded that, if I wanted to continue to have sex while we were pregnant, I must make it okay that I have sex with my child, whether female or male. I saw that it has to be okay. People do this, it's natural, right?

S: Your child gets more love.

ST: Yeah, it gets more love. So then I said, "Now, as I'm making love here, on whom should I focus my attention? Should I focus it only on my wife, or on the baby also? Or sometimes am I going to focus all my attention on the baby, my wife will just kind of be there?" I started playing around with this idea. By 6 months I was always careful with the baby in the womb, and at this point I just said "Well, here I am—right now I'm going to switch my attention from wife to the baby and I'm going to make love with the baby for a while." So I started playing around with the baby in the womb. I could feel the baby, and swing the belly from one side to the other; as I rolled her around in there I would begin to feel the whole position. I could feel where the legs were, and the little butt, and really got a sense of where the baby was in the womb. I was kind of swinging the belly around from side to side as I was making love, playing a little game. I was playing with the baby while I was having sex. Having my awareness on the baby. And I did that some—not a whole lot—but every once in a while, just for fun. And that's my story about having sex.

S: That's great. Okay, is there anything else you want to say about being a parent . . . that you've learned since Mela's birth?

ST: Well, before we ever got pregnant, before we ever considered conceiving, it was always I who didn't want to get pregnant, didn't want the responsibility of a baby, and all this stuff. Especially I didn't want to pass on all the negative conditioning and patterns that I had received from my parents. I wanted to be in a clear space, so when my baby came I wouldn't be passing on a lot of neurotic, irrational patterns to it. So I didn't want to get pregnant for years and years, didn't want the responsibility, didn't know whether I was ready to be a parent, whether I could afford a child, how it would limit me, how my life would change, what limitations I would experience because of the responsibility. Those were thoughts I had. But in the process of considering conceiving, I started letting go of a lot of that; in the process of the pregnancy I let go of a whole lot more. When the baby came, any consideration I ever had about being a parent completely vanished. I never gave another thought to any of that garbage.

S: Nothing was as important as your love for Mela.

ST: Once she was here, I was so happy and thrilled to be a parent for this being, and to share the purity of her innocence and space, it was just a total honor.

S: That's good.

ST: Any of those kinds of considerations are totally gone from me. And it's a lot of fun using my imagination and all the research that I've done over the years about child development and all the latest techniques of learning for babies (how to teach them to read before they're three years old). All these exciting things are at the leading edge of human development—they're just coming into the awareness of our society now—it's my work and hobby and love to explore. So I'm having a ball just using my creativity and watching Mela learn and develop.

S: Well, you seem like a great parent to me!

The Healing Power of Birth

The Healing Power of Birth by Rima Beth Star with contributing chapters by Steven Star.

Is birth the key to unlocking your fullest potential? In *The Healing Power of Birth* Rima Beth Star chronicles her personal discoveries through the births of her three children in 1968, 1980 and 1984. From hospital to home water births, she intimately describes the powerful shifts in consciousness she and her husband Steven chose to go through in their desire to unravel the mystery of birth and find fulfillment and joy in the process of life.

The 8 x 9 softcover edition with 100 dramatic photographs and 176 pages is available for $14.95 plus $1.25 for shipping. *Water Birth* is a 54-minute video of three of the first water births in the United States, Mela and Orien Star and Jeremy Lighthouse, interspersed with an in-depth interview of Rima and Steven Star. *Water Birth* is an extraordinary visual experience as well as a poignant discussion pointing the way toward future possibilities in human evolution. *Water Birth* is available on ½ inch VHS. Rental—$25 per showing. Purchase—$200.

Both available from Rima Beth and Steven Star, P.O. Box 161113, Austin, Texas, 78746, (512) 327-8310.

England: 36-Year-Old has her First Baby at Home—in Warm Water!

by Christiane Knight

This is only a brief report on my wonderful experience. I feel much more could be said, but I hope this short article will already be enough to generate some fruitful thinking among pregnant parents.

My pregnancy went fine. No major trouble. The few inconveniences were all greatly compensated for by the joy of creating a little baby body in my womb, and my feeling so much love for the baby coming to us.

I was confident that I would do the right thing when the time came for the actual birth if I fully understood the process, and both my husband and myself made sure that we would be ready for that.

It was so obvious to us, that Baby should be born at home. Hospitals are for illnesses or accidents—birth is a natural process and a joyful event. As a first face-to-face contact with life on Earth, we wanted Baby to come into a warm and loving atmosphere, into the place where Baby was going to live, not into an unfriendly hospital room full of strange instruments and awful smells. We wanted to be able to choose carefully the lovely midwife and to prepare the birth with her, not to have some total stranger (or worse, strangers) come to us at the moment of the birth, and perform some standard mechanics.

And I wanted to be together with my husband through the birth and then continue to stay together with him and with the baby—as we had done throughout the pregnancy. It would have been awful to have to follow hospital rules and have my husband leave me after such an emotional happening—our couple now becoming a true family.

Originally, having been warned of all the risks of home delivery for an older mother and a first baby, we accepted sadly the prospect of having to book into a hospital: we certainly would not have wanted to take the slightest risk for Baby's health or life, even though I was willing to take the risk of hemorrhage for myself! The West London Hospital was close, and had a good reputation for natural birth, Leboyer-style (without violence for the baby, not only for the mother). Anyway, neither the G.P. nor the NHS midwife would take the responsibility of delivering at home the first baby of an 'old mother' (after 30 you are definitely considered to be an old mother, regardless of your health, life-style and attitudes . . . although I truly feel younger and younger as the time passes . . . and intend to continue that way . . .).

One week before the actual due date, we had the opportunity, as part of the hospital's ante-natal classes, to visit the delivery ward. We felt then definitely that, however hard the hospital had tried—and compared to others, I am sure that the West London is very good—we did not want such surroundings for our birth. I feel that the delivery would have been more difficult in hospital because I would not have felt as comfortable as I did at home—free to do as I wished, to eat or drink what I suddenly felt like, or to listen to music.

But by now, there was only one week to go! I found some brief information about the Natural Childbirth Trust, and as it seemed in the line of what we wanted, I telephoned—to be told that a midwife had to book at least six months before the due date, and that there were only two in London anyway, and one of them was leaving on holiday just the next day! Not very encouraging.

But we are not people who give up when it is important, and to prove that miracles are possible, I was eventually put on to Belinda, a young, well-trained midwife, who herself already had a two-year-old son. Belinda agreed to re-arrange her activities and to take charge of the home birth of our baby. God bless her! And she was absolutely perfect all along.

I asked her before making the commitment what she would do, if . . . (all the problems which might occur, and I had been warned) and Belinda explained exactly how each of these could be handled. At worst, we would slow down the process of the birth and drive to the hospital.

Once the home birth was arranged, in fact, our G.P., the area NHS midwife, and the registrar we had been under at the West London, were all quite happy about it and wished us well. As Baby was eventually over two weeks overdue (apparently), we were grateful to be able to pop into the hospital three times in the final six days to monitor Baby's (very healthy) heartbeat on their machines. And our decision not to consider inducing was right, as Baby's condition and the condition of the placenta were perfect at the birth.

Eventually the contractions started on the early morning of July 7, and I could quietly continue to have a nice time at home, not worrying about when to rush to the hospital. I was, of course, in regular telephone contact with the midwife, who came at about 7 p.m., and checked then that everything was all right. She told me, too, that when the contractions got stronger, it was generally comfortable to get into a warm bath. I did . . . and as soon as I was in it, I felt so much better . . .

I began to think—I am very comfortable here in the water—Baby is also in the warm water of my womb, and has been in warm water for nine months—Leboyer puts babies back into a warm water bath just after birth to make them feel comfortable . . . . Why should I get out of the bath just to give birth?

So I asked Belinda if anyone had ever thought of that or even done it: "That's interesting you might think of that, because Dr. Odent in France has just recently started delivering babies in a pool, and they are doing the same in Russia, too. They do it in a swimming pool.

We checked that it was possible as well for us and that

there was enough space for the midwife to deliver Baby from her position at the edge of the bath, and she then said: "Well, if this is what you want, I can do it!" I must say that Belinda belongs to an organization (The Association of Radical Midwives) whose purpose it is to give back to the mothers the responsibility in the birth, and to take the mothers off their role as "patients," obeying the (generally male) specialists. At that point, I decided only to stay attuned to what I would feel was right, moment by moment. My first concern was naturally that Baby should be comfortable, and in fact I have the impression that she was sleeping through the entire process, as she only kicked twice, each time when my husband put his hand on my belly. (We got used to this behavior during the pregnancy!) The stronger the contractions became, the less question there was for me to leave the bath.

Belinda was regularly adding hot water from our electric kettle to the bath to keep it warm, while my lovely husband was giving me not only all his loving support, but also two strong arms and hands for me to squeeze while I bit very hard with all my nerves on the perfect thing (the thick rubber of a kitchen spatula!) to make sure that the tension was all only in my hands and teeth, not in the area of the womb where it would interfere with the natural, automatic work of the muscles. Terry's love was very efficient at that time, and I could not imagine giving birth to our baby without him. I am sure that the homeopathic treatment three weeks before the birth (caulophillum 30) and the lobelia herb preparation (the day of the birth) helped as well. And Belinda, herself, was perfect, being very discreet while I was following my own attunement with Baby's progress, and then guiding me very well when I asked her what I should do at the second stage.

At 10:30 Belinda had estimated that delivery would not be before 2:30 a.m. In fact the contractions went so well with the water that Baby was born at 12:30 a.m. Baby came out safely under water in the hands of the midwife and then immediately out of the water onto my belly. Our lovely Baby girl gave her brief cry of the first breath and from then on breathed gently on my breast where I could pour on to her a stream of love and words of welcome. We had talked so much to her while she was in the womb, not able to imagine her face, and now there she was!

Baby herself was born with no more than one tiny spot of blood on her cheek, and there was absolutely no distortion to the shape of her head. She had plenty of hair, and her little fingernails were already long enough to need cutting. Baby did not develop any jaundice like many babies apparently do after a few days.

We had used no drugs, no incisions had been necessary, so no stitches, and there were only two little bruises that were uncomfortable. I found that there is a natural mechanism which gets the mother to relax totally between contractions (actually "between" rather means "when the contractions were less strong," as they were nonstop after 9:30 p.m.).

The cord, which generally stops pulsating after 5 minutes, continued to pump healthily for half-an-hour, much to our surprise, at which point it was beginning to be a much weaker pulsation. The time being right, at Terry's suggestion I did the cutting myself. (I didn't feel anything of course, and Baby didn't react either.) It seemed right, as Baby was attached to me, that I would be the one to un-attach her. Afterwards Terry very happily took Baby in his arms.

The placenta, which was holding firmly as long as I was in the bath, was delivered very easily without the usual injection by squatting in the bath while letting the bath water run out—the gravity and the apparent suction of the falling water level on the weight of the placenta all seemed to help considerably, and it dropped itself into the water like a ripe fruit, entire and beautiful. Without getting out of the bath I could shower and be ready for a very welcome and deserved bed (ours!) in our next-door bedroom.

Once I was in bed, Baby was given back to me, and she sucked the precious colostrum from my breasts for one whole hour. I then slept for a very good night, Baby lying between myself and Terry, who enjoyed so much her little contented gurgles.

I am not saying that hospitals are not useful, and as each case is different, every mother has to check that all the best conditions are realized before making the decision of a home birth, and the most important of all is certainly confidence, but in case of a home birth, my experience is that the birth underwater makes everything much easier and probably much more secure.

I do not want either to give the impression that it was all dream-like pleasure. Obviously if it had not been for the birth of our baby, the same sensations would have been very painful. Only the love and the joy transformed the contractions into a "labor" rather than a "pain." I must also say that our neighbours thought there were cats around that night, as I used the screaming to release some of the tension and effort! There is indeed a tremendous energy involved and the feelings are quite spectacular, although I did not feel any ecstasy sometimes described about the birth. At the end of the first stage—around 10:30 to 11:00 p.m.—I was probably feeling about the same as mothers who ask for an epidural, but I knew that this would have prevented my pushing in due time, and might have made Baby dangerously listless, and the greatness of the work I ws accomplishing gave me such determination that I told my husband at that point: "I think I can stand it for as long as necessary." Patience went along with the strong intention to see Baby, gently and safely, and as soon as possible, OUT.

I am so grateful about this birth for myself, for Baby, and for my husband! He told me just one hour ago "Do you know, I recall the birth so many times, and I am so moved!" Our love for each other had already increased a lot during the pregnancy, and the birth itself did much more. This is why I take the time and trouble to write, although I am very busy now with our lovely daughter and the housework. I will be so pleased if more and more parents can have births in this way—and even better. Why not?

Water Baby, an Experience of Underwater Birth

by Marilyn Rodgers with Karil Daniels

(Bill Rodgers and Marilyn not only live together, but also work together in the music business. Their Allright Family Band has recorded Being With You, *which they wrote about daughter Merlinna's conception in February, 1981. Later they made a 50- minute documentary videotape about Merlinna's underwater birth, including interviews with medical personnel as well as family members. They have had their third child, a boy named Jai Michael, using water for labor and delivery and used fire meditations with his birth as well. Included at the end of this chapter is an excerpt from Marilyn's book,* **We-Creation,** *where Jai's birth experience is uniquely described. Marilyn's first child, David, who was born three months early is now nine years old, has been experiencing rebirthing throughout his childhood with very beneficial results. Marilyn is now a research assistant for a program assessing data about waterbirthed babies. Marilyn and Bill can be contacted by writing to them at 207 Derby Avenue, Derby, CT 06418.)*

While I was pregnant, I especially enjoyed bathing myself everyday. It became one of my favorite pleasures. To communicate mentally with Merlinna *in utero* became very easy in the bath, perhaps because we were sharing the same environment—she was in the womb water, and I was in the tub water.

As Merlinna's due date approached I often bathed more than once a day. Frequently I would lie in my husband Bill's arms in the warm bath, visualizing the coming birth as ideal, relaxing deeply in the certainty that my affirmations would guide us to make the best possible decisions for us, and to insure safe procedures during the birth itself. We used this time to communicate amongst the three of us, and to handle the practical and emotional aspects of birthing. Floating around in the water, yoga stretching and squatting, conscious breathing through rebirthing, all helped me to become supple and relaxed. I was very confident that this birth would be a luxurious experience for Merlinna and myself, and one in which I would be fully conscious during the entire process. I gave myself the pleasure, rest, and security I needed.

During labor I bathed early, before transition, gave myself an enema to be more comfortable, and spent time in bed getting attention and emotional support and affection from my family and friends who were present. I found Bill's love for me and constant support to be the key in easing the discomfort of labor, and am very grateful for his courage and belief in me.

Basic sexuality and sensual feelings between Bill and me shortened the time I expected to take for birth. I used our love to open up my cervix and womb. The rushes of energy became exciting this way. Ina May Gaskin is one of the only birth specialists who has elaborated on this in her work. Also in documents about primitive cultures it is explained that when a woman exceeds a two-hour period of labor, all attendants, except for her mate, are asked to leave the room. This gives the couple a chance to resolve any sexual tensions between themselves. I have heard that this loving communication works every time. Because this fact is controversial according to our traditions, it is important to collect accounts of other painless deliveries. Caring about this by writing to me about your child's birth will help to clear up the myths around childbirth. I recommend the *Loving Relationship Training* and the *Making Love Workshop* as exceptionally beneficial experiences. They are conducted in many places, just as the *Recreation Event* is. We invite you to attend one and see for yourself.

Our birth tub, which was a gift from a loving friend, measured 8 feet by 3 feet. It gave us extra room so that Bill, and our birth attendant, could be in the tub with me. I was about 8 centimeters dilated when I chose to get into the water for delivery. It was a good feeling, and relaxation spread throughout my body as I lay in the water, which was about 18 inches deep. Deep breathing and affirming, as I had practices, served me well, for I was able to enjoy myself thoroughly. I anticipated more discomfort than actually occurred. Of course, the physical comforts of water birthing gave several advantages unique only to this method. For example, when the baby began to ease down the birth canal I thought "This is where I'll get the pain," but much to my surprise even the stretch around her head was easy in the warm water, and I did not tear. It was marvelous.

The absence of directive voices and negative energies telling me to hurry it up was the best part of this birth as compared to others I've known of. We made an agreement among ourselves to handle any emergencies tactfully and calmly. Everyone remained relaxed and supportive. This aided my self-confidence and allowed me to follow my primitive birthing instincts.

Merlinna remained about three inches under the water surface for 13 minutes. It took the first five minutes of that time for her to completely emerge from the birth canal. She rested in the water for another eight minutes, relaxing and adjusting to the lights, the new position of her body, and all the other new changes. We observed her release some muscular tensions beneath the water. We were guided in the entire process by a combination of our intuition and what we had learned. While Bill carefully handled her beneath the water, and a birth attendant monitored her heartbeat and umbilical cord, we watched Merlinna's facial expression and her muscle tension to determine that she was relaxed and comfortable. When we brought her face out of the water, she began to take tiny breaths on her own. The placenta was delivered into the water about 40 minutes later. The umbilical cord pulsed for 45 minutes. We left the tub after the placenta was safely delivered. The baby, the cord, the placenta, and I were carefully transported to the bed, where we joined Bill and bonded for several hours with each other. Up until this time Bill had participated fully in the delivery and felt as much a part of this as I did. We severed the cord from the baby after 3½ hours, and later buried the fully intact placenta in our garden.

Even several months later, being in the water together is a joyful experience for our family. Our happy, healthy baby, Merlinna, is growing well and very easy to care for.

Bill and I, dedicated to having healthy, happy lives, made safety and gentleness our priority at Merlinna's delivery, even if we had to forfeit the underwater birth for more conventional methods. But that wasn't necessary. "Gentle birth" advocates believe that birth requires a lot of attention and care, and that it can also be natural, relaxed, fun, and comfortable for both the baby and the mother. We know they are right, as Merlinna's water birth was like that.

Due to my son's premature delivery four years ago, I was termed a high-risk mother. My husband and I felt that I did not have to be limited by this factor, so we investigated alternatives to the standard hospital delivery. During our research we discovered that bellydancing was really a birth ritual, that in other cultures it is common to deliver babies while in a squatting position. We learned of a variety of methods.

We saw birthing underwater as logical and advantageous for both the mother and the child. It lessens the shock of being born for the baby, eases the separation trauma, enhances the bond between the parents and the child, and has the potential of influencing the learning skills right at birth. It is true, as in any birth, that there are also risks and considerations which one should be aware of. At Merlinna's birth we experienced very wonderful results with this new method.

The advice I received from medical professionals, midwives, birth attendants, and my family regarding underwater birth was filled with caution and reserve. Of course, no one had ever had the experience, and few had even heard of it.

We made inquiries with women who had underwater

We made inquiries with women who had underwater births. We lived at Campbell Hot Springs, spending a lot of time in the natural warm waters, practicing breathing exercises, and training with Leonard Orr. Pure faith in God's work through us and the metaphysical rule that *thought is creative* washed out of our minds doubts, fears, and discouragement connected to birth and the birth process we had chosen. Detrimental emotions and physical tension were released from my body and mind through the rebirthing process. I really recommend it. Rebirthing or conscious breathing is the best way I've found to tune a person into tension, fear, and pain locked in the body, and through affirmations and the cleansing of rhythmic breathing, allows fresh new thoughts and feelings in. It's a pleasant experience, a tool for relaxation always within oneself.

In addition to rebirthing individually, Bill initiated a process with me which served us more than I ever thought possible. We have since organized the information and experience into a workshop available to anyone interested in releasing deep memories from the subconscious about birth. We highly recommend that pregnant couples have at least one session with a process like this before having birth in any way they choose. It makes a big difference in how much pain the women experience during labor. My labor felt intense but nothing like my first experience. I used the *Recreation of Birth* as a self-healing technique to open up my body and to understand my self-made limitations. This lightened up the seriousness of the birth/death trauma, yet gave balance to, and respect for, the great responsibility required of us. The *Recreation of Birth* workshop and seminar combines rebirthing, water purification and chakra meditation for as many as 12 people at a time. It is useful for non-pregnant individuals in unraveling birth and early childhood memories, social conditioning, and death beliefs. It has added happiness and health to our lives.

Recreation of Birth or *Birth Actualization* is a powerful technique that channels the energy flow through the body, opens the chakras and simulates individual birth experience.

A trained rebirther focuses on the chakras in sequential

order while the rebirthee maintains connected breathing. Assistants support the person so that they are lying on their back, floating on top of warm water. Visualizations of the appropriate chakra color by all participants enhances the cleansing process and prepares the rebirthee by sensitizing those chakras experiencing negative blocks.

Depending upon how long each rebirthee needs to feel the chakras and a natural breathing rhythm, the trained rebirther then arranges the assistants to simulate the birth canal. The rebirthee holds his breath while floating underwater in the fetal position until ready to find the birth canal and experience birth again.

To assist in completion and distribution of the *Water Baby* videotape project, Point of View Productions, through its sponsoring organization, Film Arts Foundation, 2477 Folsom Street, San Francisco, CA 94110, will gratefully accept contributions, which are totally tax-deductible. Films Arts Foundation is a 501(c)(3) charitable public foundation which administers donations to the Water Baby documentary project. To make a contribution please mail a check to Film Arts Foundation at the above address, and designate "Water Baby Project."

An information packet on water birth and the WATER BABY DOCUMENTARY PROJECT, entitled *WATER BABY: The Experience of Water Birth*, is available from Point of View Productions at 2477 Folsom St., San Francisco, CA 94110. It includes information from numerous sources about water birth and water training of infants; the work of Dr. Michel Odent, who has delivered over 120 babies in water in his hospital in Pithiviers, France, and Igor Charkovsky, the pioneering Soviet research physiologist, who developed the water birth method in the early 1960's. Compiled by video producer/director Karil Daniels, this packet is the result of in-depth research into the subject in the course of preparing the video documentary. Please send a check for $20 (which includes postage) to the address listed above.

Also, we would like to recommend Rima Beth and Steven Star, Patrick and Jia Lighthouse, and Rennie Payne-Ayers as resources within the U.S. who have given birth underwater. Each has written and photographic material to share about the births in water of their children. Also, ask for our address list of midwives and supportive birth attendants, *Recommended Reading*, which is available through Joe Moriarty, 955 W. 19th E233, Costa Masa, CA 92627 (714) 642-3919.

- *We-Creation*, Marilyn Rodgers
- *The Secret Life of the Unborn Child*, Thomas Verny, M.D.
- *God, Unlimited Mind*, Allen Michael
- *Spiritual Midwifery*, Ina May Gaskin
- *Birth Without Violence*, Frederick Leboyer
- *Rebirthing in the New Age*, Sondra Ray and Leonard Orr
- *Ideal Birth* and *I Deserve Love*, Sondra Ray
- *Physical Immortality*, Leonard Orr

For an updated version of this information send your name, address, and telephone number and we will include you on our mailing list. We encourage your involvement through our current Recreation Event, *which is described here. Also, we enjoy providing speakers for related events.*

1. Musical cassettes: "Music Is Love" and "Consciousness Village."

2. Video cassette: *WATER BABY: The Experience of Water Birth*, a 55 minute educational documentary about birth in water, shot in the U.S., France and the USSR. It provides an historical perspective on the developments leading to water birth, answers important questions many people have, interviews with medical professionals most knowledgeable about the

subject, actual water birth experiences in the U.S. and France; information on Igor Charkovsky's work in preparations for birth in water and water training of babies; and interviews with Dr. Michel Odent of France, the world's most knowledgeable medical practitioner of water birthing. For further information on the availability of this video tape, contact Karil Daniels, Point of View Productions, 2477 Folsom St., San Francisco, CA 94110.

Jai's Birth, March 16, 1985
Home Birthing and Homa
(Fire Meditation)

by Marilyn Rodgers

(Parents who advocate the underwater birthing method say that it makes the birthing process easier, the heated water helping the mother to relax, thus lessening the labor pains. The process, first developed in the Soviet Union, is said to reduce the trauma of birth for the child, the birthing environment being almost identical to that of the womb.)

We were introduced to fire as a purifying element during rebirthing training at Consciousness Village beside a great outdoor fire pit, but it was on the occasion of our son's birth that Agnihotra and Homa significantly affected us. Bill and I chose to take part in the programs offered at an Ashram in New York as preparation for the birth of our child. We are avid believers in the consciousness of divine life in the womb and so immerse ourselves in conversing with the baby in utero through water purification, conscious breathing, rebirthing, and the use of water delivery as a gentle way to share with the baby.

Coming to this place ahead of the due date comforted us and aligned us with our task of nesting for the birth. Little did we know how powerful the element of fire would be in relaxing and harmonizing ourselves and our two other children so that the highest vibrations could influence us and surround us.

Agnihotra is the basic healing fire practiced in a copper pyramid. Before hearing the Agnihotra Mantras we joined a resident daily for Agnihotra and found the fire's influence to be very profound. I recall the first time we inhaled the Agnihotra residual vapors, the effect was immediate as Bill purged and purged himself for a full day from a city diet we had been living on. The following day, he felt wonderful. Our children regarded the Agnihotra sunrise/sunset fire with awe and I felt bonded to them in a very new and special way. For me the new sensitivity to sunrise and sunset was energizing, humbling, and healing.

I truly cannot explain what actually happens from Agnihotra and Homa because it is such a subtle experience in so many ways. All I know is that it makes a tremendous difference in how I perceive my world and so I know that much about it. For example, on March 16th Jai Michael was born into a water tub about 11:30 a.m. Mild labor began about 8:00 a.m. and soon afterwards Bill called the others who were helping us along the way.

At sunrise a handful of friends were with us and the Agnihotra fire was lit. The sweet smell permeated the rooms of our home; the beautiful chants comforted and relaxed us. Bill hugged me tightly below my waist which seemed to alleviate any sensations of pain and cramping I had from the labor.

At one point when transition was coming near, Bill walked into the meditation room to find a beautiful young woman lighting the Homa fire. Regina Parks, whom neither of us know, began to chant and prepare Homa for what seemed like the most blissful and dream-like labor I could have ever experienced. Between contractions I drifted into a nirvana-like sleep, which to this day seems unexplainable because at the same time my mind felt alert and aware.

Throughout the morning *Om Tryambakam homa* fire was going on and finally when we entered the water tub for delivering the child, still the kindred fire, which warmed our hearts and the beautiful voice of Regina blazed on. It was beautiful and even though the Homa was being held two rooms away, it entered our senses.

It has been a week since the birth and the fire is remaining in our lives, an experience which seems to melt away anger, despair, and unwanted habit. It seems to rejuvenate the power, the energy, and the light of divinity. A dear friend who attended the birth asked me if she could have a tape of the music we played during the birth. She was deeply impressed by the chanting, not fully aware that it was a live session.

I recommend Homa as part of conscious home birthing. It goes along well with other wonderful benefits of having a husband who participates fully, as Bill did, and friends who share. For more information, please feel free to write to me in care of 207 Derby Avenue, Derby, CT 06418.

Water Babies and Swimming

(From You *magazine, London, England. This article was adapted by Paula Knight from* Water Babies *by Erik Sindenbladh, published by St. Martin's Press, New York, 1983.)*

In Russia, thousands of children are learning to swim before they can walk. In Moscow alone there are 71 swimming and body-hardening schools where babies are taught, almost from birth, to swim. Experiments have shown that these babies learn to stand much earlier, begin walking at six months, are rarely sick, can withstand cold and weather changes, do not have temper tantrums, sleep soundly, and are more active and brighter.

Baby swimming is already popular in the world, but this new teaching goes much further in Russia. Babies are conditioned to eat, play and *live* in and under water. Dr. Igor Charkovsky believes that a child trained to stay underwater for long periods gets a stronger start in life. "We are going to see a new kind of people, the children of the ocean. Living underwater is totally natural for a newborn baby—he's never known anything else," Dr. Charkovsky says. "After birth, a baby's weightlessness in water enables him to move around, feeling as secure and protected as he was in the waters of the womb. He can turn, dive and lie on his stomach."

Charnovsky claims that the babies he works with have, at three months, the strength and ability of one-year-olds. He suggests that if you want to make your baby better friends with the water, you should train him gently, carefully and playfully, with no sign of fear. He suggests you place orange sections and other things to eat on the bottom of the bath or pool so that the child will bend to pick them up. Put pictures on the pool wall so he will have to stay underwater to look at them. Let him imitate other water-trained children.

Perhaps the best way to start a baby associating water with something pleasant is to breastfeed him underwater, or feed him with a special baby bottle with a long teat. When the baby needs air he will stop sucking a signal for the mother to lift him to the surface for a breath of air before going down again. By the age of two months the child will be able to dive and feed himself, Dr. Charkovsky says.

There are exercises which will give a baby the feel of water. Walk just far enough into the pool so that the water reaches your stomach or chest. Lift the child in the air, toss him up, let go for a second, then catch him again. Most children think this is fun. If all goes well, let his feet splash down into the water before catching, and next time a little deeper. If the child appears tired or starts crying it is best to stop.

After awhile you can try letting the child walk on the bottom of the pool. It is a good idea to use food to stimulate him. I have built a walking chair which the child can use for support, and to which a baby bottle can be attached. You may well find that walking underwater helps your child to walk on land as early as three months. Some experts believe this is unhealthy. Perhaps for normal children. But well-trained water babies have muscles like athletes.

Russian Mothers of Water Babies May Have Laser Therapy

(This material is from the article "In Search of Superbabies" by Roy Laytner, Donald McLachian and Henry Gris that appeared in the Philadelphia Inquirer *on September 1, 1983.)*

After describing at length the work of Dr. Igor Charkovsky with his underwater newborns, the three authors relate that Charkovsky has "even higher hopes" for children yet to be born because Dr. Georgy Dzhabinava heads a team doing experimental work with lasers.

With the approval of the Soviet Academy of Sciences, Dzhabinava's team bathes babies still in the mother's womb with a low-powered Soviet "health" laser first tested in research on laboratory animals.

"It was clear from my work on animals that using the special laser reduces the danger of miscarriage, and we began working with mothers-to-be, human mothers, with a history of miscarriage, just over four years ago," Dzhabinava said.

The red laser light is applied for a few minutes at a time every second day to the pregnant mother at what Dzhabinava calls the "more vital" acupuncture points — most of them in the lower abdomen and back — but he refused to discuss this in detail. He said nearly 300 healthy babies had been born to mothers who had never had a successful pregnancy before.

"There is general agreement among all the experts who have observed the procedure and examined the babies regularly since birth that they are unusually robust and remarkably free of childhood ailments like coughs and colds.

"Most of the mothers came to us because they had a history of miscarriage. Their only concern was to have a normal, healthy baby. We have been successful in every single case. This therapy is enabling women to carry babies they would have probably lost to full term."

An Underwater Baby
Nineteen Years Later!

My friend Mikela told me she had met a young man who was born underwater nineteen years ago in the Cayman Islands. I was immediately intrigued, wondering how I could ever meet him and interview him for this book. A miracle happened about nine months later. This young man just "happened" to come to Florida and "happened" to be where I was. So I had the privilege of talking to him by the pool along the canal. It seemed appropriate to have water all around.

His name is Neville Von Schleffenberg. He struck me as a very sweet, intelligent and handsome young man, totally relaxed and happy. He has a European name because he was adopted by a Baron. "Quite an easy and abundant life he has created," I thought, "just what I would expect for a water baby who had an easy birth."

His mother was a 23-year-old unmarried woman who was swimming at the time she went into labor. There was no transportation available to get her to a hospital, and when the uncle and grandmother came, they found her on the edge of the beach with her legs in water. Two women held her as her baby, Neville, came out underwater. He remained underwater for 4 to 5 minutes in the ocean, which was amazing to me, since it was "accidental." His mother, who must have been very intuitive, said "Leave him there" as if she knew he wanted and needed that time. When he came up his breathing was clear and free—there was no slapping. The cord was cut on the beach. It was a short labor and easy delivery, and that is just how he is—easy-going, to say the least.

Neville grew up on the beach. Of course he loved swimming as a baby. He was always in the water. His mother could not keep him out of it. She had to change his clothes as often as seven times a day, he told me. Sometimes his dog would try to stop him from constantly going in the ocean, but to no avail.

At 8½ he was adopted by the Baron Von Schleffenberg. I was much impressed with their relationship. The two of them were just about the easiest people to get to know that I have ever met.

Of course, you can imagine how easy it is for Neville to free dive. He can bring up a 30-pound fish in four minutes from 104 feet! And he loves doing yoga underwater, relaxing there for more than three minutes at a time.

When I met Neville, his young wife was pregnant, and we talked to her about having their baby underwater.

Contacts

For more information on underwater birth, you will find names and addresses in Appendix II.

Gentle Birthing Project

If you would like the support of a group I would suggest you contact the Gentle Birthing Project of Portland, Oregon. Below is a statement drawn up by the group of which I am a consultant. Perhaps you will also help us begin other groups in America, such as in your community.

What is the Gentle Birthing Project?

The purpose of the project is to give birth a higher state of consciousness and to promote our evolution as peaceful human beings by focusing our awareness on birth, which includes conception, intrauterine experience, delivery, postpartum and parenting. We are committed to everyone knowing that a child is a conscious being and to be responsible for that knowledge.

The project is a multi-disciplinary association of health care practitioners, birthing teachers, counselors, midwives, parents and other supporting personnel and lay persons interested and committed to gentle birthing. We have modeled our practice after experts and pioneers in gentle birthing and wholism. Frederick Leboyer, M.D., Michel Odent, M.D., Lewis Mehl, M.D., PhD, Gayle Peterson, MSSW, LCSW, and Sondra Ray, R.N., MPH and rebirthing specialist, are consultants to the Project.

Together we have developed an approach designed to lower infant mortality and to deliver provably healthier and better adjusted infants. Early observations have shown promise in the following areas: higher intelligence, better family relationships, and enhanced immune systems. We anticipate a significant increase in home births until hospital programs can accommodate this approach.

If you are interested in participating in this project in any way, we would love to hear from you as soon as possible. Write to us and tell us specifically how you would like to contribute.

Write to:

Robert P. Doubhton, M.D., and
Athena Neelly, R.N./L.M.T.
The Gentle Birthing Project
1744 NW 32nd Avenue
Portland, Oregon 97210

or call: (503) 227-7352

Part IV

Rearing a Child

The best environment I can imagine in which to raise a child is one of unconditional love and unconditional trust. Trust that your child is safe in God and the world. Trust that it will do what is good and appropriate.

If a parent is constantly worried that a child will be bad or hurt, it probably will be. The child telepathically acts out the parents' thoughts. Remember that the Bible says: "What you fear comes upon you." In metaphysics we say "What you fear, you attract."

You may "think" you are loving a child by worrying about it, but the child will feel your worry and assume there is something dangerous to worry about. Actually, *there is no danger unless you think there is.*

Setting a good example is always the best way to raise a child. Disapproval destroys self-esteem. If you must disapprove, at least disapprove only of the actions, not of the being. Even this must be done tactfully. Why is the child doing something to warrant disapproval anyway? What is it trying to tell you? Children are not inherently bad. They are inherently good, and their so-called bad behavior is a reflection of what is going on in the psychic space. Always remember, children are your gurus. If they are acting "bad," chances are they are acting out your suppressed negative thoughts so that you can see them. Are you willing to see them? The best thing to do is to go sit by yourself and take a look at your own mind. Perhaps if you were to change your thoughts and breathe, the baby's mental state would be totally different in a second. Think about it.

Children are like thermometers that give you a reading of what is going on in the subconscious of those around them.

Because we as children may have received a lot of disapproval in the form of "discipline" does not mean that this is the best way to raise children. There is a tendency to "go on automatic" and unconsciously respond to your children just as your parents responded to you, even though you may have thought you would do otherwise. (The typical statement is "I'll never raise my kids the way I was raised." And yet, when I did research on the battered child syndrome, I was amazed to find that 100 percent of the parents who battered their children had been battered themselves as a child.) Be aware. Don't get even with your parents by taking it out on your own kids. This will cause you unending heartache. Forgive your parents for the way they reared you, if you did not like it. We must, after all, take complete responsibility for choosing our parents, and for the fact that they were probably responding to our negative subconscious commands.

Let's have children who are wanted.

Let's prepare ourselves for them.

Let's have children of enlightened parents.

Let's remember that anyone can be enlightened.

Let's have children growing up in an atmosphere of love, positiveness and health.

Let's give up hate, greed, fear, worry, doubt, and sickness.

Please do not leave this book thinking that all the things in it are only for some, or only for the privileged, or only for the rich, and not for you too. You can have anything if you want it. Please do not assume that these things are hard. They are easy and natural. Going against the natural is hard. What is available to one of us is available to all of us. The *Course in Miracles* says that "All differences are temporary." Each of us can have it all. We are each tuned into God and Infinite Intelligence. You can have the perfect ideal birth. You can create it yourself the way you want.

These are simply some of my ideas. Please send me yours. Thank you.

Is There an Ideal Attitude?

I do feel that the babies who are coming through in this present energy of enlightenment are very high souls. They should be treated with great respect. We are smart to learn from them. I always consider a new baby to be my guru. Surely this is a good attitude to have as a parent.

As mentioned before, children act out the subconscious minds of their parents. This is because they are very sensitive to emotions and feel everything. It is also because they want resolution of suppressed feelings. In metaphysics we know the principle that "Love takes upon itself your negative so you can see it more clearly."

Children will, out of love, act out your suppressed negative thoughts so you can see them and be healed. So when your child is acting weird, don't get angry. Don't rush to punish. Don't rush to blame. Don't give verbal abuse. Stop and take a look at *your* feelings. Is the child expressing something *you* need to express? Are you angry? Are you stuffing it? Children find this intolerable. They will expose everything. So you better be ready for the total truth!

The attitude I recommend is humility. Give up the idea that you are going to be a heavy "disciplinarian." Give your child a good example. Never put your child down. Avoid, at all costs, smashing the spirit and self-esteem of your child. Avoid over-parenting.

Talk to your child right from the beginning with extreme gentleness. Listen for its answer. Until it can speak, it will answer you psychically. Let natural telepathy develop. Let your child teach you what it wants and needs. You will both be happy. Always remember that Infinite Intelligence is operating.

Always remember that a child senses
what is expected of him and goes into
agreement with that.

If a parent expects that the child will get
hurt and constantly warns of "danger," the child
will probably get hurt. The parent expects it.

If a parent expects that the child will be
unable to cope, cranky or uncooperative, that
is probably the result that will occur.

Expect your child to be happy, cooperative
obedient, and easy to be with!

Accelerating the Intelligence Potential of Your Child

Joseph and Jitsuko Susedik, of Concord, Ohio, have four children. All of them are geniuses, having 150-plus IQs. The Susediks began an intensive tutoring program for them that started even before birth. They talked right to the womb, teaching alphabet, phonics and social studies. The parents, who claim their IQs are just average, routinely talked to each fetus as if it were a child in the room. Joseph claims the girls said Mama and Papa at three weeks, not clearly but recognizably. By nine months all four girls were reading flash cards and personalized primers. Jitsuko, who taught English in her native Japan, claims that her teaching method is based on pure love. She taught whenever her children wanted to learn.

Experts have differing opinions about the results of accelerated learning. This is a very controversial issue. To examine all sides, I recommend checking your library for information on "superlearning." There are also courses for parents on the subject of increasing your baby's intelligence. Books are available on subjects like "How to Teach Your Baby to Read" and "Teaching your Baby Math."

For more information and guidance correspond with The Institute for the Achievement of Human Potential, 8801 Stenton Avenue, Philadelphia, PA 19118.

However, *be aware* that Joseph Chilton Pearce, in *Magical Child* (New York: Bantam, 1980) warns of the possible dangers of this kind of thing. During an interview with *Mothering* magazine (Spring 1985), Dr. Pearce was asked to what he attributed the demise of childhood that we see in modern-day society. This was his answer:

There were several major things that happened to children within a single generation, beginning around World War II. Novel obstetrical practices disrupted the bonding process between mothers and infants.

At the same time, we violated the first seven years of life as the absolute sacrosanct period for leaving the child alone and allowing him to be a child. We began to encroach upon this period with academic training. Rudolph Steiner predicted that this would lead to severe difficulties such as premature sexuality, but no one paid any attention to him.

Formal operational thinking, abstract logic, and semantic thinking are adolescent developments; when you force them on the child too soon, you also inaugurate signals connected with adolescence and puberty. When those signals mix in with those designed to unfold from age four to seven, the child receives mixed signals and is in a state of extreme confusion.

We disrupt the preparatory periods of development when we force abstract learning on the child prematurely.

The message is clear: Do not force a child to adapt to patterns which do not match the biological stage of the child's developmental process.

I would highly recommend all future parents study this brilliant book by Dr. Pearce, *Magical Child* (New York: Bantam, 1980).

The Importance of the
Spiritual Family

The ideal would be to expose the child to a "spiritual family" right from the beginning. This may or may not include your natural family. It could include a church, if one is careful not to impose the doctrine of separation and guilt. To me, of course, the ideal would be to expose the child to a group of Immortalists and to the rebirthing community where the people involved had worked out the Five Biggies, (the five major areas of subconscious influence):

1. The Birth Trauma
2. Parental Disapproval Syndrome
3. Specific Negatives
4. The Unconscious Death Urge
5. Other Lifetimes

This would provide the child with a tremendously free and nourishing attitude in which it did not have limiting thoughts of pain, suffering, disease and death. I feel this would invite the most aliveness into your child. I would recommend the enlightened books as part of the growth process, to be read at home in front of the child from a very early age. (See Appendix, Recommended Reading.)

The ideal home atmosphere would be that of a temple. It is not absolutely necessary to go to church to have a temple. A child would thrive in an atmosphere of holy rituals, prayer time, sharing time (family therapy), and Rebirthing sessions. Having the infant present from the beginning at these daily rituals will infinitely enhance its life and your life.

Recommended Daily Prayer Ritual

I. OPENING—Reading out loud from the *Course in Miracles* text or other favorite scripture.

II. THANKSGIVING—Stating to another or others what one is grateful for.

III. FORGIVENESS—"Who or what I want to forgive today is . . ." "Who I want to be forgiven by is . . ."

IV. PETITION—Stating to another or others "What I would like to ask for today is . . ." "What I need is . . ."

V. CLOSING—Reading to self or aloud to another or others a daily lesson from *Course in Miracles* daily lesson or other scripture.

I guarantee that this process will produce miracles for your family. Imagine starting life like this!

Part V

A Tribute to my Mother

On My Birth and Rearing

I love the fact that from the very beginning, my mother really wanted me. I was wanted and planned. In fact, she was so tuned in to me in the womb, that she actually got my telepathic request: I wanted to be born at home. It was very unusual at that time to have a home birth. My older sister had been born in a hospital. It was expected, and popular, to have a typical hospital birth. However, because my mother was careful to bond with me *prenatally* and to communicate with me, she acknowledged my desires as a being. I wanted to be born at home no matter what. I acknowledge her for following her intuition. (In many rebirthings I have actually "remembered" trying to communicate this desire to my mother from the womb. She got it, and I appreciate it.)

During the labor, my mom walked around the house and actually whistled during the contractions. This was more comfortable for me, inside, because it relaxed her. To this day, I go into bliss when I hear someone whistle.

At my delivery I had both a family doctor and a midwife, who was my mother's best friend. I felt very loved having them both there. My dad was there too, as were some relatives. It was a very "social" event! I have always been, as a result, a very social person. Of course, after my birth I had the benefit of being with mother and bonding completely without interruption. I was not taken away to a nursery, and so I did not have to go through separation anxiety. I feel this greatly contributed to my present self-esteem and resulting success.

I also loved the way my mother reared me. When I was a child, she gave me total space. I felt free to grow up without a lot of heavy rules, disapproval or strict discipline. I did not need discipline, I just needed a good example, and she gave me that. (The alternative to discipline is setting a good example.) My mother also trusted me completely as a being, and I felt this. She seemed to be saying telepathically, from the beginning, "I trust you. You are good and I know you know what you are doing. I give you space to be yourself." I felt this at a very early age and, as a result, I wanted to live up to her highest thoughts about me. I wanted never to disappoint her or myself. I was a good child, eager to be a responsible being like she was.

Later, when my father died while I was in high school, I became a rebel. His death was intolerable to me and I reacted in an extreme way. Even this my mother seemed to understand. She accepted all the strange things I did and did not lecture me. She just prayed for me and gave me unconditional love. She was exactly the right mother for me in order to do the work I am doing.

I do not remember my mother ever complaining. I do not remember my parents ever fighting. This I appreciate greatly. I think it was a reflection of my mother's positive thinking and her constant positive attitude. She always thought positively, no matter what, and let go of any upset very fast. Even when my father died, and I knew she must be devastated (since he was the only man she had ever loved) she seemed to handle it exceptionally well. I wondered how she could take it. I was having trouble mastering my feelings about it, so I finally asked her how she could be so strong and recover so fast.

Her answer stunned me. She replied "Well, Sondra, I had you girls. Some women can't even have any children." She taught me, without knowing it, always to reach for a higher thought.

My mother always had *faith* in me and that worked. She always acted as if I could take care of myself so she was never guilty of over-parenting. This enabled me to be very expressive and creative and to feel happy, completely alive, and free to be me.

Mother's Day, 1983

APPENDIX I

Some Medical Implications Supporting Water Birth

by Barbara Keller

The child from birth must be regarded as a being possessed of an important mental life and we must treat him accordingly. The first care given to the newborn baby, overriding all others, must be a care for his mental life and not just for his bodily life, which is the rule today.[1]

Maria Montessori

For generations, medical science denied what ancient people knew so well—that the newborn child and even the unborn child has an aware consciousness. Now laboratory scientists are verifying that the infant can feel and understand his feelings, translate a sensation into an emotion and attach a cognitive significance to it.

Dr. Thomas Verny gives a summary of the sensory development of the fetus in his book *The Secret Life of the Unborn Child.*:

> *By his fifth week, . . . studies show that (the unborn child) is already developing an amazingly complex repertoire of reflex actions. By his eighth week, he is not only moving his head, arms and trunk easily, he has already fashioned these movements into a primitive body language—expressing his likes and dislikes with well-placed jerks and kicks . . . .*
>
> *Facial expressions take a little longer . . . to master. By his fourth month, the unborn child can frown, squint, and grimace.*
>
> *Four to eight weeks later, he is as sensitive to touch as any one-year-old.*
>
> *From the sixteenth week in utero, he is very sensitive*

to light. And while that (sunlight) does not disturb him,
shining a light directly on his mother's stomach does.[2]

Studies in neurology have proven that consciousness exists
in utero and also pinpoints the time it begins.* Sometime between weeks 28 and 32, the brain's neural circuits, which
relay messages from the brain to various parts of the body,
become just as advanced as those of a newborn baby. At the
same time, the cerebral cortex, most complex part of the
brain, matures enough to support consciousness.[3]

Other studies show that the unborn infant listens all the
time, especially to the sound that dominates his world, the
maternal heartbeat. Some interesting research on the significance of the sounds heard by the unborn child was presented
at the International Conference on Infant Studies, 1984, by
R. K. Penneton and A. J. DeCasper of the University of
North Carolina. Their study showed that newborn babies of
one to three days prefer the sound of interuterine heartbeats
to male speech heard postnatally and the voice of their
mothers over that of other females. They also found that
newborn babies prefer to hear a nursery rhyme read aloud
by their mothers during the pregnancy more than a novel
rhyme she had never recited.[4]

This research suggests that unborn infants learn about specific features of sound before birth, which include not only
properties of speech, but also elements of the maternal voice
and of non-speech sounds, such as the maternal heartbeat.
This work supports a prenatal hypothesis that the reinforc-
ing effects of certain postnatal events is a function of their
similarity to events experienced prenatally and shows that
the newborn remembers prenatal events.

Research like this is clinical proof of observations from
LSD psychotherapy that suggest the unborn child experiences distrubances of pregnancy, such as chronic anxiety,
tensions and emotional stress of the mother and that these
prenatal memories are stored in the subconscious.[5]

Another avalanche of research on the cognitive abilities of

the newborn child is exploding the myths of the past—myths on which traditional obstetrics are still based:

Before 1960, when Hebbs *The Organization of Behavior* dominated most theories of perceptual development, many observers believed that the newborn baby does not possess innate dispositions to perceive the world in particular ways. It was even suggested that the infant had to *learn* to perceive shapes. "We now know that the infant is able to perceive hue, shape, pitch, contour, movement, and selected olfactory and taste dimensions and that his attention is selectively recruited to particular values of these dimensions."[6]

Dr. Frederick Leboyer, the pioneering French obstetrician who questioned and revised accepted birth practices, is very aware of the newborn's dilemma: being totally aware and yet treated as if he were not.

> *Some people see the newborn's cries as a manifestation of triumphant life, others as cries of torture. All I can tell you is that I have seen and listened to a lot of newborns. It becomes evident that what we have there is a kind of heavy sobbing . . . like an unlimited sadness . . . . There is no doubt that the suffering stems from the huge contrasts between what the infant has been through before and what he experiences at birth. But also, I am convinced that the lack of understanding with which the newborns are welcomed is one of the prime causes.*[7]

Perhaps obstetricians choose to assume a lack of consciousness in newborns because few adults can spontaneously recall uterine life or the experience of birth. We may now have a clue as to why those deeply memorable experiences are not available to adult consciousness.

During labor and birth, the mother's body secrets the hormone, oxytocin, to induce contractions and lactation. The hormone also passes through the placenta into the baby's body. Recent experiments have shown that oxytocin produces amnesia in laboratory animals. Even trained animals forget their ability to perform tasks they know well when exposed to the hormone. Nature seems to have provided a means of sublimating to the subconscious the memory of birthing our highly evolved, and therefore large, brains through a relatively small passage. This does not mean, however, that the preconscious memory is without its influence on later personality and behavior.

Because we now understand the fetus has a conscious awareness at the moment of birth, and because we recognize the birth experience resonates throughout one's lifetime, we are now challenged with developing humane and appropriate delivery methods. One such approach may be using warm water as a medium for birth.

There would be no tears, there would be no sadness, if the newborn were born into the warm waters of a birthing pool, an environment similar to the amniotic sac. If the infant were allowed to slide from womb into warm water, the trauma would have a chance to heal; the infant's body would have time to adjust to freedom and an independent existence before being exposed to the pressure of gravity and other hazards of terrestrial life.

We are not saying that birth can ever be an easy passage. The transition from womb to world will always be a difficult, arduous one. Dr. Verny describes the experience vividly:

> Birth . . . is the first prolonged emotional and physical shock the child undergoes, and he never quite forgets it. He experiences moments of incredible sensual pleasure—moments when every inch of his body is washed by warm maternal fluids and massaged by maternal muscles. These moments, however, alternate with others of great pain and fear. Even in the best of circumstances, birth reverberates through the child's body like a seismic shock of earthquake proportions.[8]

And these experiences come at a time when the baby is totally exhausted from the birth ordeal and his delicate organs are going through enormous changes to adapt to independent, extra-uterine life. The maintenance of body temperature and the final development of certain internal organs require large amounts of oxygen, yet the newborn's lungs have never been used before and do not expand for many hours after birth.

"The most perilous period in infancy," according to Dr. Clement A. Smith, "is the neonatal period of two weeks after birth." He adds:

> The perils which infants face during and immediately after birth are not now especially those of infection; they are difficulties in the onset of respiration, and the hazards of obstetrical accidents.
>
> This is a time during which life is more dynamic than static, for in no other equally brief span of existence do such profound alterations and adjustments occur as in the weeks, days and even the moments following birth.[9]

At birth, developing kidneys, heart, liver, endocrine and respiratory systems need large amounts of oxygen to help the infant's body adapt to extra-uterine life and independent existence:

> Oxygen is needed for the maintenance of metabolism in every cell in the body. Any block to the supply of oxygen to a cell will cause the infant's metabolism to grind to a halt. This means the death of the cell. The failure of metabolism causes such by-products as carbon dioxide and organic acids to accumulate. The cells in the brain are particularly affected by the lack of oxygen and the next most crucial are those of the liver and kidneys, although all cells of the body are vulnerable.

Yet when babies are born into the colder air of the delivery room, whether in hospital or home, their bodies lose heat rapidly because the temperature of the room can be 30 degrees lower than that of the womb. (70 degrees compared to 101 degrees). The infant must waste precious oxygen

234

simply to maintain body temperature when it is urgently needed for other functions:

> Human infants are homeotherms. To survive they must maintain body temperature at a constant level in spite of environmental changes. In adults, shivering contributes to heat production. In the newborn infant, however, heat production comes essentially from a release of chemical bonds during metabolism (non-shivering thermogenesis). Approximately 60 percent of the energy released by metabolic activity is cast off in the form of heat. Basal matabolism, however, does not produce enough heat to compensate for the heavy losses in the unprotected environment of the delivery room.
>
> Compensation for the heat lost on delivery requires great increases in metabolic activity, which in turn utilize large amounts of oxygen and energy (glucose).
>
> Metabolic rate change may be measured by the rate of oxygen consumption. The higher the metabolic rate, the more oxygen required by the infant. For instance, a decrease in body temperature of just 6.3 degrees F requires a 100 percent increase in oxygen consumption for more than one and a half hours just to replace the heat lost during the temperature drop.
>
> Healthy, full-term babies cared for in an environment of 89.6 to 93 degrees F use oxygen at the rate of 5.4 ml/kg/minute. After exposure to environmental temperatures of 77 degrees F their oxygen consumption goes to 9.3 ml/kg/minute.[10]

In other words, if the temperature of the delivery room is 75 degrees F, the infant requires a 400 percent increase in oxygen consumption for six hours, just to replace the heat lost in adjusting to the 25 degree temperature difference between womb and world!

Many conditions of the newborn considered by obstetricians as harmless may indeed indicate oxygen starvation. As Dr. Harold Abramson has noted:

Misinterpretation of observations has resulted from incomplete knowledge of the physiology of labor. Many of the present conclusions concerning fetal physiology immediately before birth are drawn from biochemical conditions that exist at delivery, on the assumption that they represent the normal in utero environment. As a consequence, the process of labor and delivery has been neglected as a most likely source of biochemical asphyxia.[11]

There is much clinical evidence of inadequate oxygen in newborns. For instance, cyanosis, the slightly bluish discoloration of the skin due to reduced hemoglobin in the blood, is so commonplace it is considered normal. The infant's surface blood vessels are constricted in an attempt to conserve the heat lost upon exposure to the cooler air of the delivery room:

Cyanosis of the skin is present immediately after birth, but with the onset of respiration the color improves rapidly. Cyanosis of the hands and feet, acrocyanosis and perioral cyanosis may persist for a variable length of time and should not be considered abnormal, but rather the result of local peripheral vascular changes.[12]

Acidosis in a mild form is also considered by obstetricians to be normal in newborn babies.

When oxygen levels are inadequate to maintain normal glucose metabolism, anaerobic metabolism of glycogen occurs. One of the consequences of this anaerobic process is an increase in lactic acid production, which leads to clinical acidosis.

Most newborn infants have a mild acidosis which is of both metabolic and respiratory origins and which ordinarily needs no therapy . . . . Acidosis may rapidly increase in severity in infants in whom respiration is not established.[13]

If the oxygen shortage is severe enough to cause cyanosis or even a mild form of acidosis in many infants, it is probably severe enough to cause oxygen depletion in the kidneys, liver and brain. The functioning of these organs could thus be permanently affected. Particular concern should be given to the brain because:

> *Of all the parts of the body, the brain is the most susceptible to insult, but maintenance of its normal function is most essential for survival. Unlike any other tissue, it cannot be repaired. Virtually the entire complement of cells are present at birth and if any are lost, they are not replaced. During a human life span, the brain is at high risk at two periods: in old age . . . and in the perinatal period when even an intact blood supply may not provide adequate oxygen or nutrients.*[14]

There can, therefore, be little doubt that many brain cells are potentially lost during traditional births due to oxygen deprivation because the newborn's lungs are simply not ready to supply the tremendous amounts needed to maintain body temperature as well as supply the organs. In fact,

> *There is evidence to indicate that complete expansion of the lungs of the newborn may not occur with the first few breaths but may be delayed for several days or even a week or more.*

Any pulmonary situation that decreases the functional surface area of the lungs or the alveolar-capillary membranes decreases the efficiency of external respiration. Such a pulmonary situation exists at birth because the lungs of the newborn are more like sponges than the balloons they will become. Indeed they are sponges filled with amniotic fluid that must be expelled before normal respiration can begin.

Thus the newborn is thrust into an environment perceived as hostile and must struggle to survive the loss of oxygen. The circumstances could easily be reversed if the baby simply emerged into warm fluid. Conservation of heat means conservation of energy. When heat and energy are conserved by keeping the infant in warm water until respiration is firmly established, as in underwater birthing, the amount of oxygen needed to maintain homeostasis is much less; therefore, more oxygen is available to the organs, especially the vulnerable brain and the still forming kidneys and liver that need such large amounts of it.

Experiments with newborns in water have been taking place in Russia for over twenty years; it is said that the ancient Egyptians used water birthing for future Pharoahs and prophets. The first recorded water birth in this country took place on October 28, 1980, when Jeremy Lighthouse was born to his parents Jia and Patrick Lighthouse in a hot tub filled with salt water at 101 degrees, the temperature of his mother's womb.

Jeremy stayed totally submerged under water for a full twenty minutes after birth with his umbilical cord attached, sending him oxygen, nutrients and hormones. His umbilical cord was still intact when he surfaced and began to breathe through his lungs for the first time. For the next twenty minutes, during which the cord remained intact, he probably received oxygen from two sources.

Sheltered from the full impact of gravity by the buoyant salt water, Jia was able to give birth under water with a minimum of pain and stress after a labor that lasted only two hours. The water assists the tissues of the vaginal canal to stretch, so there is usually no tearing of the perineum in underwater births even after previous episiotomes. Under water, contractions are more efficient and less painful and labor is quicker.

Because the umbilical cord does not dry out and constrict in water, as it does when exposed to air, it can remain useful longer assuming the placenta does not detach from the lining of the uterus. When that happens, the exchange of oxygen and nutrients in the maternal-infant blood flow is terminated. How long the placenta will remain viable varies, but once the baby is out of the womb, it will begin to detach soon. The uterus will also begin to contract to decrease the mother's blood loss which also decreases the circulation to the placenta.

If there are no problems with placental and/or cord function, and the baby remains submerged for any length of time, the mother must be extremely sensitive to what is happening in her body and the infant *must* be carefully monitored. The flow of blood through the cord may continue for some time, but on the other hand, it may slow down so much that the baby must begin to breathe through his lungs. In most cases, even after the baby's head is brought to the surface and lung breathing begins, he will still be receiving some placental blood and thus have TWO life-support systems going. In fact, even in hospital air births, where the cord is exposed to the withering and constricting effects of air, a strong placental transfusion of maternal blood through the uncut cord for up to five minutes is normal.

According to Dr. Carey Teasdale, a California obstetrician who has delivered several babies under water, there is some problem with placenta and/or cord malfunction in about 20 percent of all births, which makes total submersion of the baby riskier. Basically, she says, there are three situations that will cause the placenta to stop functioning prematurely and thus halt the flow of maternal blood:

(1) When the umbilical cord is compressed during the second stage of labor;

(2) When the function of the placenta is borderline to begin with, as in diabetic mothers, mothers with poor nutrition or smoking mothers (who are all to much at-risk to deliver out of hospital anyway);

(3) When the placenta separates from the wall of the uterus immediately, as in an abruption, or if the cord is around the baby's neck and tugging on the placenta.[15]

In these cases, of course, the infant must be brought to the surface immediately to begin lung breathing. The problem arises when it is difficult to determine if the placenta and cord are functioning adequately.

Whether the baby is completely submerged under water or not, Apgar scoring could begin immediately, just as in air births. Dr. Teasdale feels:

> *Reflexes can be checked by touching the nose, mouth, or eyelid; the baby should grimace. After the body is out, the grasp reflex on both hands and feet should be checked frequently and should remain strong. Muscle tone is also the same as on land; arms and legs should be flexed and the baby should resist a pull to straighten the arm or leg. The baby should not be limp or flacid.*[16]

Since the initial underwater birth, it has been discovered that all the many benefits to the newborn can be accomplished within two to five minutes. At subsequent births therefore, parents have raised the baby's head above the water within that time frame. Even with his head out of the water, the rest of the baby's body is being protected from heat loss in the water and most of the available oxygen can go to the organs that need it most. And the baby is experiencing the soothing effects of an environment so similar to the womb that he does not feel the shock of adjusting to terrestrial life with the same intensity as in dry births. The bouyant factor of the salt water protects the delicate tissues and cells of his body from the pressure of gravity during this critical period of adjustment.

The unrestricted freedom of movement the newborn has in the birthing pool must feel like heaven after the confines of the womb, especially after the arduous passage through the vaginal canal! Jeremy's parents reported that, after a few moments of tension on his face his expression during the whole twenty minutes he was in the water was calm and relaxed and an atmosphere of peace enveloped the whole family.

Because the world feels very welcoming and much like his previous home there is no wall of anguish between prenatal and postnatal life for the water-born baby. He will more easily recall life in the womb, and therefore his life will be all of one piece, instead of fragmented.

What a contrast between the peaceful serenity of the water-birthed baby's entrance into the world and the traditionally birthed baby's. Here, from a book on nursing procedures, is a description of the state of a normal, healthy, full-term baby immediately after birth:

> *For the first 15 minutes or so (after), the baby normally undergoes rapid respiration, grunting, tachycardia (fast heart beat), flaring of the rib cage with intercoastal indrawing, rapid fall in body temperature, hypertonus (tension) and exploratory behavior (i.e., flailing of the arms in all directions as the baby attempts to orient himself in space), all associated, of course, with a good cry.* During this time, there is considerable secretion of oral mucus, so don't think that the initial suctioning is all that necessary.[17]

It is considered normal for the infant's pulse to be anywhere from 125 to 180 beats per minute, due to abrupt exposure to air that increases cardiac output.

Jeremy's condition after birth was a stark contrast to the rapid heart beat, the lowered body temperature, the tachycardia, and the disorganized, chaotic movements of the dry-birthed baby.

> *During his twenty-minute swim, he "sometimes kicked, sometimes floated, with his father's assistance, sometimes slept, just as in his mother's womb. He went through two series of chest heaves as he expelled small amounts of the fluids which collected in the lungs. The flow was always positive, from the lungs out. Jeremy never once tried to inhale water . . . Jeremy's futher had one hand on the baby's heart, one hand monitoring his pulse rate and/or one hand on the cord at all times. The baby's heart never slowed down or speeded up.*[18]

About twenty minutes after his birth, his mother passed a blood clot, alerting her to the fact that the placenta was detaching and that it was time for Jeremy to surface so he could begin breathing on his own. Jeremy's father raised him, placed him on his mother's chest with his head tipped to one side to assist in clearing out any remaining mucus, but apparently Jeremy had evacuated it all under water, as none appeared after he surfaced. Transition to lung breathing was very smooth. Jia says:

> *Jeremy never took one big gulp of air; he merely played with breathing. He would gurgle, take a breath, pause and the whole time his umbilical cord was pulsing at the same strong rate so there was no urgency for him to breath continuously immediately.*[19]

Since the moist cords of water-birthed babies remain functioning for a significantly longer time than air-birthed babies, we may gain some perspective on the potentials for the baby by observing newborns whose cords were not clamped off for up to five minutes. We can assume any benefits accrued would be exaggerated over time.

Though the time the cord was left intact varied considerably in the studies and none of them discussed cords that functioned as long as Jia's, "early" clamping means within 15 to 30 seconds after birth, while "late" clamping means leaving the cord intact for from 3 to 5 minutes after birth.

In one study the early-clamped group contained more than three times as many depressed infants as the late-clamped group. The depressed infants showed signs of perinatal asphyxia and possible respiratory distress syndrome.

> *Careful studies using I-tagged albumin have shown that the red blood cell volume is higher in late-clamped infants, compared with the early-clamped, and remains so for the first five days of life.*[20]

Since it is the red blood cells, not the plasma, that carry

and deliver oxygen, early clamping of the cord apparently deprives the newborn infant of much precious oxygen.

The oxygen deficiency in the group of early-clamped infants showed up in another way:

> Early clamping of the cord leads to a significantly lower skin temperature over the palms and the heels of the newborn infants compared with the late clamping. These findings were attributed to a reduction of peripheral blood flow to the skin in the absence of a placental transfusion.[21]

There are even more benefits to late-clamping:

> Urine flow, glomular filtration rate, PAH clearance and effective renal blood flow are all lower in early-clamped infants compared to late-clamped infants during the first twelve hours after birth. Late-clamped infants achieved a reduction in blood volume after birth due to high urinary output along with low sodium excretion.[22]

This data shows that the kidneys of the late-clamped infants function better than those of the early-clamped infants. Dr. Smith may have the clue as to why:

> Although the kidney is morphologically an essentially complete organ at (full-term) birth, most of its functions appear to require a longer interval than the arbitrary two weeks of the neonatal period for development from the limited capacities at birth to full competence. The most rapid progress is that earliest made.[23]

The "most rapid progress is that earliest made" because in the early moments after birth, the infant still has the mother's hormones and enzymes necessary for kidney development in his system. It seems essential for kidney function that the umbilical cord be clamped as late as possible. This would imply that the water-birthed baby, whose wet cord remains operational, may receive even greater benefits.

According to the following report, late-clamped infants also benefit from receiving more of a transfusion of blood than early-clamped infants:

> In 1963, Usher and co-workers drew attention to the fact that the wide range of values for blood volume reported in the full-term newborn, ranging from 70 to 150 ml/per kg of body weight, was related to whether the cord was clamped immediately or not. It was calculated that the volume of placental transfusion could amount to as much as 60 percent of the baby's blood volume or 166 ml in a 350-gram infant.[24]

> Measurements made by Stembara and his colleagues using a thermodilution technique in full-term newborns indicate that umbilical blood flow continues at a rate of about 75 ml/kg per minute up to 60 seconds after birth and thereafter decreases sharply.[25]

The sharp decrease in umbilical blood flow after the first 60 seconds after birth may be due to the umbilical cord, upon exposure to air, beginning to wither and constrict and the flow of blood being impeded. This does not happen to the cord when the baby is born into water, as moisture keeps the cord from constricting, so the blood flow could conceivably continue for a longer time. (However, the decrease may be due to the placenta's detaching from the uterus, which of course could also happen in underwater births.)

Late-clamped, dry-birthed babies can have problems that water babies do not have. For example, when the cord is left unsevered for even as long as five minutes in dry births, physicians worry that the newborn will receive *too much* blood from the placenta. *Placental overload*, as this condition is called, occurs because the newborn is held at a level lower than the mother's introitus (vaginal opening). This is done to create more pressure in the cord and prevent it from becoming constricted by keeping the blood flowing downwards. But because the blood flow is going in one direction only (from mother to baby), the baby cannot expel wastes through the umbilical cord and yet cannot depend on his own excretory system either. The infant's body becomes overloaded with blood.

There is little danger of placental overload happening to water-birthed babies because there is no need to create more pressure in the cord by holding the infant below the mother's introitus. The infant can float in the water at the same level as the mother and, because the water keeps the cord viable, the blood flows just as freely from the baby back to the mother through the umbilical veins as it does from the mother to the baby through the umbilical artery. Thus any excess blood in the baby will be eliminated by the baby, just as it is *in utero*.

Yet another problem for late-clamped, dry-birthed babies that does not apply to water-birthed babies has to do with fluid loss and kidney function. The study comparing late-clamped to early-clamped infants showed that, although red blood cell volume is about 60 percent higher in late-clamped infants, their fluid loss is greater:

> *Total blood volume in early-clamped infants remains fairly constant in the first four hours, but decreases over this period in late-clamped infants by 30 mg/kg. This is due to loss of plasma and is accompanied by a rise in hematocrit from around 48 percent at birth to 64 percent at four hours. This fluid loss appears to be rapid, with 20 percent of the blood volume moving out of the intravascular space during the first 8 to 15 minutes of life.*[26]

The more rapid loss of fluids in the late-clamped infants (dry-birthed) is probably due to their superior renal function. They eliminate more fluid than early-clamped babies because their kidneys function better. At any rate, since it is the red blood cells and not the plasma that carry oxygen, the plasma loss is not a problem to *water-birthed* babies, because they cannot become dehydrated in water!

In water birthing, there is also little danger of supine hypotension syndrome:

> *In supine hypotension syndrome, a sudden drop in maternal blood pressure can occur when a pregnant woman lies on her back. The blood return to the heart is decreased by the weight of the uterus on the inferior vena cava and the decreased circulating blood volume results in a lowering of the blood pressure. If the maternal hypotension is severe or prolonged, the baby may experience hypoxia and acidosis.*
>
> *A drop in maternal blood pressure also presents a potential threat to the fetus. Systemic hypotension causes a decrease in the volume of blood available for placental circulation; hence it decreases proportionately the supply of oxygen available to the infant and the means for removing fetal carbon dioxide. During labor, maternal hypotention can occur as a result of . . . supine hypotention syndrome.[27]*

In the tub of water the mother may take any position that feels comfortable, which would never be on her back! Most women who have given birth under water say that kneeling, leaning forward in a crouching position or a semi-reclined position against her partner is most comfortable.

The worry that infections could occur more easily under water is not founded in theory or experience. Prolonged labor, which is more characteristic of dry birthing than water birthing, is more likely to be the cause of infections than exposure to the warm, salty water used in birthing pools.

> *Infections occuring during the birth process are usually secondary to invasion of the mother's genital tract by a variety of different organisms . . . . Infection in the mother result from the ascent of vaginal bacteria into the amniotic cavity. Transmission to the fetus occurs*

through its mouth and nose . . . .Statistically, mothers
with prolonged labor—that is, more than 12 hours—
particularly with prematurely ruptured membranes, ap-
pear to be more likely to develop intrauterine infec-
tions.[28]

In water birthing, labor is usually more efficient and quicker than in dry births, so infections are less likely to occur. Moreover, infections are more common in hospitals, where mothers and babies are exposed to a wide variety of unfamiliar and dangerous germs than in a home where both are already immune to their own germs. No instance of infection has been reported in America, Russia or France, where Dr. Michel Odent, Head of Obstetrics, has caught nearly 200 babies in the labor pool at the General Hospital of Pithiviers.

Even though birthing in water at first seems unnatural, given a little thought it becomes obviously natural. Everyone of us lives in a kind of primaeval ocean that we carry around inside. Every cell in our bodies floats in salt water in which nourishment is dissolved and waste products are excreted. In spite of civilization and millions of years on land, human life is still created and, in one sense, is still spent in the waters of the sea!

REFERENCES

1. Montessori, Maria, M.D. *The Absorbent Mind*, Dell, 1967, 136 – 46.
2. Verny, Thomas, M.D. *The Secret Life of the Unborn Child*, Dell, 1981, 36 – 37.
3. Purpora, Dominic. "Consciousness," *Behavior Today*, June 2, 1975, 494.
4. Penneton, R.K. and A.J. DeCasper. "Newborns Prefer Intrauterine Heartbeat Sounds to Male Voices," *Infant Behavior and Development: an International and Interdisciplinary Journal* Vol. 7, Special ICIS issue, Ablex Publishing Company, Norwood, N.J., April 1984, 281.

5. Grof, Stanislov, M.D. *Realms of the Human Unconscious*, Viking 1975, 105.

6. Kagan, Jerome, Ph.D "Psychological Research on Human Infancy: An Evaluative Summary," William T. Grant Foundation Publication, New York, 7.

7. Bela Bohus, et al. "Oxytocin, Vasopressin, and Memory: Opposite Effects on Consolidation and Retrieval Processes." *Brain Research*, 157: 414–17, 1978.

8. Verny, Op. Cit., 98.

9 Grof, Op. Cit., 96–98.

10. Montessori, Op. Cit., 68.

11. Abramson, Harold, M.D., *Resuscitation of the Newborn Infant*, C.V. Mosley, 1966. 202.

12. Robert, Florence Bright, R.N., M.N. *Perinatal Nursing: Care of Newborns and Their Families*, McGraw-Hill, 1977, 39–41.

13. Abramson, Harold, M.D., Op. Cit., 199.

14. Wilson, J. Robert, M.D. *Management of Obstetrical Difficulties*, 6th edition, C.V. Mosley, 626.

15. Goodwin, James W. and John O. Godde. *Perinatal Medicine: The Basic Science Underlying Medical Practice*, Williams and Wilkins, 1976, 239.

16. Wilson, J. Robert, Op. Cit., 630.

17. Bada, H.S., et al. "Intracranial Pressure and Cerebral Arterial Pulsatile Flow Measurements in Neonatal Intraventricular Hemorrhage," *Journal of Pediatrics*, 100, 291–96, 1982.

18. Lind, J., L. Stern and C. Wegelius. Human Fetal and Neonatal Circulation," Charles C. Thomas, Publisher, Springfield, Illinois, 1964, 37–40.

19. Tennes, K. and D. Carter. "Plasma Cortisol Levels and Behavioral States in Early Infancy," *Psychosomatic Medicine*, 35, 121–28, 1973.

20. Huch, A. and R. Huch. "Transcutaneous, Noninvasive Monitoring of PO_2, *Hospital Practice*, 11, 43–52, 1976.

21. Teasdale, Carrie, M.D. "Underwater Birth—A Dangerous Fad or the Ultimate in Gentle Birthing?" *International Childbirth Education Association News*, May 1984, 9–10.

23. McKilligan, Helen R., M.D. *The First Day of Life: Principles of Neonatal Nursing*, Springer Publications, New York, 1970, 27.

24. Lighthouse, Jia and Patrick. "Underwater Birth: Great Beginnings," a recording by Lighthouse Productions, 463 E. Street, Olivenhain, CA 92024.
25. Goodwin, Op. Cit., 217.
26. Goodwin, Op. Cit., 216.
27. Goodwin, Op. Cit., 217.
28. Goodwin, Ibid.
29. Smith, Clement A., M.D. *Physiology of the Newborn Infant*, Charles S. Thomas, Publisher, 1959, 323.
30. Goodwin, Op. Cit., 215.
31. Goodwin, Op. Cit., 217.
32. Wilson, Ibid.
33. Robert, Op. Cit., 30.
34. Abramson, Op. Cit., 25.
35. Montessori, Op. Cit., 136–46.
36. Gunnar, Megan R. et al. "Coping with Stress in the Neonatal Period: Deep Sleep and Plasma Cortisol Levels During Recovery From Circumcision," *Infant Behavior and Development*, April 1984, 150.
37. Leboyer, Frederick, M.D. "Birth Experiences," *Birth*, edited by Catherine Milinaire and Joseph Berger, M.D. Harmony.
38. Montessori, Ibid.
39. Sidenbladh, Erik, "Wasser Babies," *Geburt and Entwicklung in unserem Urelement*, Synthesis Verlag S Gerken, Lutterbecks Busch 9, D-4300, Essen 1, Germany, 1982.
40. Myer, J.R. "The Great Pyramid. Birthplace or Tomb?" *A Look at the Unusual*, W.E. Davis, Hancock, Wisconsin, May 1984.
41. Montessori, Ibid.
42. Montessori, Ibid.
43. Raphael. *The Starseed Transmissions: An Extraterrestrial Report*, Uni-Sun, Publisher, Kansas City, 1982, 36.

Homeopathy:
Pre-Conception and Pregnancy

by Dr. Daniel J. Dixon,
Naturopathic Physician

Homeopathy is a safe and natural treatment for pregnant women. Unlike many drugs which easily cross the placental barrier with side effects for the fetus homeopathic remedies are non- toxic for both the mother and the fetus. Many common problems of pregnancy such as morning sickness, varicose veins, constipation, urinary complaints, insomnia, etc. are effectively treated homeopathically. Homeopathy is useful for labor difficulties, post-partum stresses such as depression and also for problems of breast feeding.

A woman's state of health may undergo dramatic changes during pregnancy. If her vital force or defense mechanism is strong she will usually feel a sense of well being during pregnancy. If it is weak her chronic disease tendencies will tend to emerge.

Homeopathy is a 200 year old system of natural medicine. Its roots are found in the writings of Hippocrates and Paracelsus but Samuel Hahnemann, a German physician, formulated the principles and laws of cure into a formal therapeutic system at the end of the eighteenth century. Homeopathy is a non-toxic therapy using natural substances to stimulate the body to heal itself. It is a healing art that recognizes that the spiritual, mental and emotional levels are affected when a person is sick—not just the physical. Homeopathy treats the whole person rather than suppressing specific symptoms. Symptoms are interpreted — not as the problem—but as the body's best effort to heal itself. And homeopathic remedies are given to support that process. Homeopathy can effectively treat a wide range of health problems from acute ailments to complex chronic disease. It can help prevent recurrence of disease and work toward establishing and maintaining a high level of health without having to depend on drugs, special diets, or other treatments.

Homeopathy in the United States today is not a profession unto itself as it was in the nineteenth and early twentieth century. It is a therapeutic specialty that doctors and health professionals of different disciplines may choose to practice after years of post-graduate study.

In Homeopathy the term 'miasm' is used to refer to an inherited predisposition to disease that may be passed from generation to generation and establishes an underlying cause for disease if the right set of circumstances arise later in life. The strength or weakness of an individual's natural defenses is related to the intensity of this miasmatic influence.

The predisposition of a child will lie somewhere between that of the two parents and is also related to the state of health of the parents at the time of his or her conception. It is for this reason that it is very important for prospective parents to increase their own level of well being—not after the mother is pregnant—but prior to conception. Their level of health is a result of their own miasmatic background and other factors at the time they conceive their child such as stress, nutrition, amount of rest, their thoughts, the presence or absence of drugs or alcohol in their system, etc. If they are conscious of this and maintain their health during childbearing years it can save their children much ill health in the future. If the parents have health problems and have the opportunity to be treated homeopathically a few months prior to conception their own level of health can be raised and consequently their own miasms or predispositions will not be passed on to the next generation. Classical or constitutional homeopathy is one of the few ways that this may be accomplished.

Homeopathy is the truth about medicine and will have far reaching implications in the future. Because it affects such a deep level of the individual it can contribute greatly to the integrated spiritual, mental/emotional, and physical well being of people. It can strengthen and harmonize the life force and creative urges in the individual. With increased public awareness and greater numbers of qualified practitioners homeopathy will help to heal the planet.

February, 1986
Seattle, Washington

APPENDIX II

Contacts

For more information on birth, underwater birth, and rebirthing, contact:

Steve and Rima Star (who delivered their baby underwater)
P.O. Box 161113
Austin, Texas 78746
(512) 327-8310

Patrick and Jia Lighthouse (who delivered the first known underwater baby in the United States)
c/o P.O. Box 727
Molokai, HI 96748
(808) 558-8982

Binnie Dansby (preganacy and birth consultant and rebirther—contact for lectures, seminars and video presentations)
2265 Westwood Boulevard, #305
Los Angeles, California 90064
(213) 312-9111

In Europe, contact:
Dr. Michel Odent (author of *Birth Reborn*)
Hosp. de Pithiviers
47 Avenue de la Republique
45300 Pithiviers, France

In New Zealand, contact:
Estelle Myers
Rainbow Dolphin Center
R.D. 3, Whatau Road
Keri, Keri, New Zealand

For information on the Loving Relationships Training contact:
LRT National
145 West 87th Street
New York, NY 10024
(212) 799-8324

or in Europe:

Diana Roberts
9d Claverton Street
London SW1, England
01 630 1501

For information about Rolfing, contact:
Boulder Center for Structural Integration
Box 1868
Boulder, CO 80306
(303) 449-5903

What You Read During Pregnancy

Did you ever stop to think about what your mother might have been reading while you were in the womb, and how that affected you? I rebirthed a friend recently who told me her mother had been reading a book about the Holocaust during her pregnancy. This was hardly the input she wanted to have while coming in. It was very disruptive. How about reading only positive, spiritual, metaphysical books? In the following bibliography are a few books I would recommend, and then after that you'll find a more complete listing of suggested readings available from Life Unlimited, an excellent source for books and tapes to support your personal and spiritual growth.

Another source of information and products related to ideal birth is:

The Whole Birth Catalogue
Commanda, Ontario POH 1J0
Canada

Bibliography

Pregnancy and Childbirth: The Complete Guide for a New Life
Tracy Hotchner, 1979

An unbiased, concise summary of the important facts in almost every area related to childbearing. Topics range from making decisions about parenthood, through all aspects of pregnancy (including sexual and emotional problems), the birth of the baby, complications of pregnancy and birth, breastfeeding, and post-partum care of the family.

The Experience of Breastfeeding
Sheila Kitzinger, 1979

This comprehensive book deals with feelings as well as techniques of breastfeeding covering such areas as: breastmilk composition, breast function, initiation of breastfeeding, infant needs, difficulties, effects of pollutants in the environment, relationships and sex and the breastfeeding woman, the older baby and other social and psychological aspects of breastfeeding.

The Birth Diary
Sheila Kitzinger, photos Suzanne Arms, 1981

A beautiful addition to Kitzinger's writings, this book offers the new mother an exciting document of her own pregnancy and birth. Describes what to expect physically and emotionally, as well as the joys, problems and preparation involved in each stage. Ample room for personal notes.

The Complete Book of Pregnancy and Childbirth
Sheila Kitzinger, 1980

Well-illustrated, very comprehensive book by this well-known author.

Life Before Birth
Ashley Montagu, 1977

Helpful guide on pre-natal health and well-being of the unborn child. Discusses effects on fetus of nutrition, maternal emotions and the birth process.

The Secret Life of the Unborn Child
Thomas Verny, with John Kelly, 1981

An exciting look at the intellectual and emotional growth of the unborn child. Verny's unique findings show evidence of the fetus as a feeling, experiencing, remembering being.

The Experience of Childbirth
Sheila Kitzinger, 1978

Classic on the Kitzinger method, which integrates the physical, social and psychological aspects of childbirth. Practical preparation guide, and more.

Birth Without Violence
Frederick Leboyer, 1975

Revolutionary presentation of birth as experienced by the newborn. Exquisite photos. Introduction of the Leboyer method, known for the low lights, and quiet birth setting.

Special Delivery: The Complete Guide to Informed Birth
Rahima Baldwin, 1979

Complete resource for parents seeking home birth with spiritual perspective. Prenatal care, backup, supplies, preparation, attendants, labor, complications, and examining the newborn. Photo illustrated.

Spiritual Midwifery
Ina May Gaskin, 1978

Self-trained midwives on this communal farm in Tennessee guide parents to joyous natural births. Statistics of over 1000 farm births, midwifery manual, many beautiful birth accounts.

The Womanly Art of Breastfeeding
La Leche League International, 1982

A practical manual for nursing mothers, offering lots of instruction and supportive advice. New edition.

Other Books of Interest:

Loving Hands, by Fredric Leboyer.
Birth Reborn, by Michel Odent.
Water Babies, by Erik Sidenbladh.
Education Begins Before Birth, by Master Omraan Michael Aivanhov.
Born to Live, by Gladys T. McGarey, M.D.
Childbirth With Insight, by Elizabeth Noble.
Essential Exercises for the Childbearing Year, by Elizabeth Noble.
Transformation Through Birth, by Claudia Panuthos.
Birthing Normally, by Gayle Peterson.
Pregnancy As Healing: Volumes I & II, by Gayle Peterson & Lewis Mehl.
Prenatal Bonding, by Eve Bowen.
Women: Torch of the Future, by Torkom Saraydarian.
The Magical Child, by Joseph Chilton Pearce.
Special Delivery, by Rahima Baldwin.
Pregnant Feelings, by Rahima Baldwin & Terra Palmarini.

The Value of Reading
and Listening

The following books and tapes contain some of the most valuable ideas to be found anywhere. I encourage you to use these products to further your growth and success. Reading and listening is a wonderful and effective way to use the suggestion principle. Take charge of our life—deliberately build the consciousness you want now by reading and listening to these and other positive products. Surround yourself with good ideas.

I suggest that you pick one or more of these books and tapes that appeal to you and use it to expand your success. Get into the habit of self-improvement. A positive and enlightened consciousness is your most valuable possession.

Recommended Reading

I Deserve Love
Sondra Ray

$6.95, paper, 128 pages
Celestial Arts, Berkeley, CA
Love, sex, and relationships. Using affirmations to have what you want, and to expand your self-esteem. Affirmations are "positive thoughts you hold in mind to produce desired results." Why and how affirmations work is the powerful topic of this book. Through writing and stating affirmations, thought patterns become progressively more positive. You then tune in to the "universal consciousness," attracting those on higher and higher vibration levels. Affirmations such as "I deserve love," and "I deserve sexual pleasure," are shown to work in a matter of days. This is strikingly illustrated by the various case studies which Sondra presents throughout the book. The book is filled with positive ideas on sex, love, relationships and self-esteem.

The Only Diet There Is
Sondra Ray

$6.95, paper, 156 pages
Celestial Arts, Berkeley, CA
"Driving up the California coast one glorious winter day, Sondra
Ray read me the text of this book. It was stunning. The message
was so simple, so true, I was amazed it hadn't been written
before. As often with Sondra's ideas, I volunteered to be the first
'subject,' the first tried-and tested 'experiment.' Would this really
work? The next day I began this unusual diet. Life has never been
quite the same. By the end of the week, I'd lost several pounds
but, more important, I was so in love with life and myself I had
the self-worth to create a beautiful body. Within one month I
had lost fifteen pounds, achieving my perfect body weight. The
theory is simple. Thought we might think it is our negative
eating habits that have kept us unattractive and unhealthy, it is
really our negative thoughts and feelings."
From the Preface by Linda Thistle, Ph.D.

This book is about much more than weight and dieting. It is
about improving your relationship with your self and your
body.

Celebration of Breath
Sondra Ray

$7.95, paper, 204 pages
Celestial Arts, Berkeley, CA
This book picks up where *Rebirthing in the New Age* leaves off.
Sondra shares new advancements in Rebirthing. Spiritual En-
lightenment, Healing and related ideas. Highly recommended for
anyone interested in Rebirthing.

Rebirthing in the New Age
Leonard Orr and Sondra Ray

$9.95, paper, 320 pages
Celestial Arts, Berkeley, CA
Filled with insights and information on rebirthing, spiritual enlightenment, the affirmation technique, physical immortality, prosperity, and much more. This was the first book written about Rebirthing. The first section of the book is the story of the discovery and evolution of the rebirthing process.

Ideal Birth
Sondra Ray

$8.95, paper, 300 pages
This book discusses the importance of "bonding" between mother and baby while the infant is still in the womb. It is felt a person's emotional, psychological, and intellectual development begins in the womb so a loving relationship and an awareness of the needs of the fetus are paramount.

The therapeutic value of water has extended to the birth process. In this latest book from Sondra Ray, the premise that water minimizes the stress experienced by an infant at birth (and also calms the mother) is advanced through the retelling of the labor experience of a woman who is a rebirther and lecturer on the subject.

Sondra Ray, a leading rebirther and therapist, is author of I Deserve Love, Loving Relationships, The Only Diet There Is, Celebration of Breath, and co-author with Leonard Orr of Rebirthing in the New Age.

Drinking the Divine
Sondra Ray

$12.95, spiral binding, 192 pages
Celestial Arts, Berkeley, CA
This is Sondra's own exploration of her experience and use of the spiritual work *A Course in Miracles*. She has integrated her use

of it into her own daily practice and into the workshops and trainings which she does around the world. She has developed a workbook of daily exercises for an entire year based on her own interpretations of the *Course.*

Spiritual Psychology

A Course in Miracles

$40.00, three volumes in hardcover
$25.00 single paperback volume
Foundation for Inner Peace, Farmington, NY
The *Course* is designed to undo the experience of separation from God which is the source of all negative experiences in life. From the Introduction: "This is a course in miracles. It is a required course. Only the time you take it is voluntary. Free will does not mean that you can elect what you want to take at a given time. The *course* does not aim at teaching the meaning of love, for that is beyond what can be taught. It does aim, however, at removing the blocks to the awareness of love's presence, which is your natural inheritance. The opposite of love is fear, but what is all-encompassing can have no opposite. This course therefore can be summed up very simply this way: Nothing real can be threatened. Nothing unreal exits. Herein lies the Peace of God."
Volume 1: Text. Volume 2: Workbook for Students. Volume 3: Manual for Teachers.

Choose Once Again, Selections from *A Course in Miracles*
Foundation for Inner Peace

$6.95, paper, 128 pages
Celestial Arts, Berkeley, CA
The most beautiful portions of *A Course in Miracles* have been selected and arranged here for you.

Love Is Letting Go of Fear
Gerald Jampolsky

$5.95, paper, 128 pages
Celestial Arts, Berkeley, CA
Based on material from *A Course in Miracles*. The lessons contained in this book will teach you to let go of fear and remember that our very essence is love. *Love Is Letting Go of Fear* provides daily exercises that give a direct and effective way to bring about individual transformation.

From Here to Greater Happiness
Joel and Champion Teutsch

$2.95, paper, 176 pages
Price/Stern/Sloan, Los Angeles, CA
Joel Teutsch was one of Leonard Orr's teachers. This book gives everyone a look at how the mind works to create your own reality. Examples are shown of personal laws (the patterns that control your life) in action. The final section presents 12 ideas which can be used to transform your life for greater happiness and success.

The Creative Process in the Individual
Thomas Troward

$9.95 cloth
Dodd, Mead & Co., New York, NY
This is an excellent book on metaphysics—how life works. Other books by the same author are good, too. (Doré Lectures; Edinburgh Lectures; Bible Mystery & Bible Meaning)

Your Inner Child of the Past
Hugh Missildine

$3.50, paper
Simon and Schuster, New York, NY

This is a clear, loving psychological book about childhood. It gives case histories which you can use to locate your own childhood patterns.

Spiritual Psychology
Jim Morningstar, Ph.D.

$8.00, paper, 180 pages
Spiritual Psychology Press, Milwaukee, WI
A brilliant synthesis of Contemporary Psychology, Holistic Health, and Modern Metaphysics. An integration of the body, mind, and spirit for the new age.

Rebirthing

(See also: *Rebirthing in the New Age, Celebration of Birth*)

Rebirthing: The Science of Enjoying All Your Life
Phil Laut

$7.95, paper
Trinity Publications, Hollywood, CA
This book describes how rebirthing works in a simple and detailed way. Contents include: The truth about being human; Rebirthing; How to create your reality; Your past and you; Immortalist philosophy; Your future and you.

Rebirthing for Health Professionals
Dr. Eve Jones

$1.00, pamphlet, 10 pages
Life Unlimited, Fair Oaks, CA
An excellent presentation of Rebirthing from a medical/ scientific viewpoint.

Birth Without Violence
Dr. Frederic Leboyer

$11.95, cloth, 128 pages
Random House, Westminister, MD
Birth from the baby's viewpoint. Reading this book can help you remember your own birth and the first (nonverbal) conclusions you made about life. Beautifully written and illustrated with photographs of blissful and aware babies. This book is required reading for the Rebirthing process. It is also an excellent book for anyone who is planning on being involved in the birth of a child. Rediscover the divine child within you.

The Secret Life of the Unborn Child
Dr. Thomas Verny, M.D.

$7.95, paper
Doubleday & Co., Garden City, NY
Synthesizing for the first time the latest findings from all scientific disciplines dealing with the unborn, including Dr. Verny's pioneering work in prenatal psychology. *The Secret Life of the Unborn Child* demonstrates that from the sixth month of intrauterine life (and sometimes even earlier) the unborn child is a feeling, experiencing, remembering being who responds to and is deeply influenced by his environment.

Money and Prosperity

Money Is My Friend
Phil Laut

$5.00, paper
Trinity publications, Hollywood, CA
"One of the best books available about prosperity consciousness." The author probes every area of life that could be

blocking the reader from reaching his full potential. This book covers the topic of "money in abundance" in depth.

Moneylove
Jerry Gillies

$2.95, paper
Warner Books, New York, NY
Particularly good for freeing up your attitudes about money.

The Richest Man in Babylon
George Clason

$2.95, paper, 160 pages
Bantam Books, New York, NY
A wonderful primer on the four laws of wealth. Recommended at money seminars as the best basic book about money. Written in parables. "A lean purse is easier to cure than to endure."

Physical Immortality

Physical Immortality
Leonard Orr

$9.95, paper, 80 pages
Celestial Arts, Berkeley, CA
In depth discussion of immortalist philosophy. An account of the immortal master Herakhan Baba in India. Socological implications of physical immortality.

The Door of Everything
Ruby Nelson

$3.95, paper, 180 pages
DeVorss & Co., Marina del Rey, CA
A wonderful statement of Immortalist Philosophy.

The Immortalist
Alan Harrington

$5.95, paper, 316 pages
Celestial Arts, Berkeley, CA
An alternative to the belief systems that accept and educate people for inevitable death. It proposes that "the time has come for man to get rid of the intimidating gods in his own head, to grow up out of his cosmic inferiority complex, to bring his disguised desire for eternal life into the open and go after what he really wants — the only state he will settle for — divinity." "Mr. Harrington may have written the most important book of our time."
—Gore Vidal

Ye Are Gods
Annalee Skarin

$4.95, paper
DeVorss & Co., Marina del Rey, CA
Annalee Skarin recognized the message of life eternal-physical immortality through study of the Bible. Her book is an extremely powerful affirmation of life and the unlimited power of God through and in any person. She has overcome death to the point that she can appear and disappear at will. She is the author of the book *Beyond Mortal Boundaries* which is now out of print.

The Life and Teachings of the Masters of the Far East
Baird Spalding

$4.00 per volume, 5 volumes, paper
DeVorss & Co., Marina del Rey, CA
An account of American scientists who visited and lived with immortal masters in the Himalayas around the turn of the century. From the introduction:
"During our stay—3½ years—we contacted the great masters of the Himilayas. . . They permitted us to enter into their lives intimately, and we were thus able to see the actual workings of the Great Law as demonstrated by them. . . They supply everything

268

needed for their daily wants directly from the universe, including food, clothing, and money. They have so far overcome death that many of them now living are over 500 years old. . ." Full of uplifting ideas. They explain how they do it and how you can do the same.

Psychological Immortality
Jerry Gillies

$12.95, cloth, 256 pages
Life Unlimited, Fair Oaks, CA
A synthesis of science and immortalist philosophy. Exercises to expand aliveness. It includes the latest scientific research on the causes and prevention of aging and death, and the lastest information on the power of your consciousness.

Hariakhan Baba: Known, Unknown
Hari Dass

$2.50, paper
Sri Rama Foundation, Davis, CA
Hariakhan Baba is an immortal master of India. He has appeared for thousands of years throughout the Himalayan districts. This book contains stories, interviews and photographs never before published in the West; 18 photographs.

Autobiography of a Yogi
Paramahansa Yogananda

$2.95, paper, 592 pages
Self Realization Fellowship, Los Angeles, CA
This famous classic tells the life story of Paramahansa Yogananda. It includes stories about many of the great masters and saints of India, such as Hariakhan Baba, and of the miracles they performed.

Weight and Healing Your Body

(See also: *The Only Diet There Is* by Sondra Ray)

Heal Your Body
Louise Hay

$2.35, pamphlet, 17 pages
Louise Hay, Los Angeles, CA
This is the complete text of the booklet which is partially reprinted in chapter 12 of *Celebration of Breath*. The attitudes and feelings that cause many physical "illnesses" are revealed. An example of a healing treatment thru the use of loving positive thoughts is given.

Suggested Listening

Tapes by Sondra Ray

Your Ideal Loving Relationship
Sondra Ray/Raphael

$10.00
Approximately 45 Minutes/side Cassette Tape
Produced by Life Unlimited (see address below)
Here is the perfect companion to Sondra's book. Just lie back, relax, switch on the tape player, and listen to incredibly beautiful music accompanied by the highest available positive thoughts on Loving Relationships. This is an affirmations tape, intended for repeated listening. I suggest playing it while lying down, bathing, driving, or anytime you can relax and let it slide into your subconscious. The music was created by Raphael specifically for these affirmations. Those of you who have heard him perform know that he has the ability to capture the exact vibration of an idea, and transmit it through music. Each of his compositions

with me uniquely fit the meaning of the affirmations, and blend perfectly into an irresistible harmonious whole. The affirmations cover a full range of relationship ideas — attracting and keeping your perfect partner, fulfillment and depth in the relationship, successful communication, harmony, and support, getting exactly what you want, resolving old patterns, and more. Both sides are identical.

Your Ideal Relationship with Sex
Sondra Ray

$10.00
Approximately 24 Minutes/side Cassette Tape
(Produced by Life Unlimited (see address below)
Sexual pleasure is your divine birthright. This tape is designed by Sondra to free your mind of limiting beliefs about sex, such as guilt, fear, inhibition, etc. Through the use of affirmations, results you can expect include the ability to relax and be yourself freely in sex, freedom to honor your own desires and standards regarding sex. Clarity about your purpose in sex, increased intensity and duration of sexual pleasure, being more comfortable with your sexuality and sensuality and certainty that pleasure, and sex, are good, and divinely approved. Raphael has created a sensual musical background especially for these affirmations. Both sides are identical.

Your Ideal Relationship With Your Body And Weight
Sondra Ray

$10.00
Approximately 24 Minutes/side Cassette Tape
Produced by Life Unlimited (see address below)
This affirmation tape trains your mind to have power over your body and what your body does with the food you eat. You establish the goal of your perfect weight and use those affirmations to bring it into being. You will also learn to love, or expand your love, for your body. The tape includes a specially composed musical background by Raphael. Both sides are identical.

Your Ideal Relationship with Money
Sondra Ray

$10.00
Approximately 30 Minutes/side Cassette Tape
Produced by Life Unlimited (see address below)
Fill your mind with prosperity the easy way with this beautiful affirmations tape. The tape contains the highest and best ideas about prosperity and money in affirmation form. Repetitive listening (with an open mind) will free you from all financial limitation by bringing up and dissolving any ideas in conflict with the positive ideas presented. The masterful musical background by Raphael makes listening a pleasure and helps to slide the ideas right into your subconscious. This is a wonderful way to practice the prosperity ideas presented in some of our other products. Both sides are identical.

Rebirthing as a Business
Sondra Ray and Phil Laut

$12.00
90-Minute Cassette
Produced by Life Unlimited (see address below)
This is a training tape for people interested in becoming Rebirthers. It is a wonderful way to learn about Rebirthing in detail and I recommend it to anyone who is being rebirthed or interested in being rebirthed.

Wet Rebirthing
Sondra Ray and Phil Laut

$12.00
90-Minute Cassette
Produced by Life Unlimited (see address below)
Wet Rebirthing is an advanced rebirthing method which uses immersion in water. This tape explains wet rebirthing in detail. Both hot and cold water rebirthing are discussed.

Rebirthing for Health Professionals
Dr. Eve Jones

$5.00, Approximately 30 Minutes/total Cassette Tape
Published by Life Unlimited (see address below)
An excellent presentation of Rebirthing from a medical/scientific
viewpoint. This is the same as the pamphlet in voice form.

Recreating Your Ideal Birth
Rima Beth Star and Glen Smyly

$15.00
30 Minutes each side
Produced by Life Unlimited (see address below)
This is a cassette tape of a guided visualization process with a
music background. It starts with relaxation, leading you back in
time prior to conception. You then picture your conception,
growth in the womb, birth and post birth experiences in the way
you would like them to have been. Side Two is filled with affirmations on forgiveness and healing of your birth experience.

Birth Separation
Barrie Konicov

$12.00
45 Minutes each side.
The birth experience for most people is very traumatic. It can be
the source of many physical ailments. This tape will help correct
your breathing and release the negative feelings of your past that
surround your birth. This hypnotic tape is designed for repeated
use.

Physical Immortality

Unravelling the Birth/Death Cycle
Leonard Orr

$18.00
Two Tape Set, Approximately 2 Hours (Live)
Produced by Life Unlimited (see address below)
An excellent tape on 2 of the 5 Biggies: Birth and Death. Why do people die? There is an unconscious link between the patterns set up at birth and the time and circumstances of your death. Death is not inevitable. This powerful tape explores the possibility of unravelling your own programming toward death. You will experience greater aliveness now as you reclaim control over the destiny of your physical body. Depression, failure and hopelessness will become things of the past. Explore youthing as an alternative to aging. Family patterns. The unconscious death urge and how it operates. Affirmations. One of Leonard's best.

Weight and Healing Your Body

(See also: *Your Ideal Relationship with Your Body and Weight* by Sondra Ray)

How to Obtain These Books and Tapes

The prices listed above are accurate at the time of this printing, and may change. Many of the books are available in bookstores. To make it easy for you to get these products, I have arranged with LIFE UNLIMITED to carry all of the books and tapes listed above. They have many more excellent titles as well. Write or call for a free catalog:

LIFE UNLIMITED
8125 SUNSET AVENUE, SUITE #204
FAIR OAKS, CA 95628
(916) 967-8442

NOTE: one letter code for each book:

- **I** for I DESERVE LOVE
- **O** for ONLY DIET
- **R** for REBIRTHING IN NEW AGE
- **C** for CELEBRATION OF BREATH
- **L** for LOVING RELATIONSHIPS
- **B** for IDEAL BIRTH
- **D** for DRINKING THE DIVINE

To order the products listed above:

1. List the titles you want, totalling at least $10.00.
2. Include your name and shipping address.
3. Add $2.00 for shipping and handling + $.35 per title.
4. California residents add sales tax.
5. Make your check or money order to Life Unlimited.
   (Checks must be drawn on a U.S. bank.)

or call and charge it (Visa or Mastercard). There is a 4% handling fee on telephone orders.

Readers interested in obtaining information on Rebirthing or LRT should write the following addresses:

For information concerning LRT and Sondra Ray:

> LRT
> 145 West 87th Street
> New York, NY 10024
> (212) 799-7323 — 7324

For information concerning Rebirthing in your area call:

> (212) 799-7324.

Films

Birth, a film produced by Helen Brew, with commentary by R.D. Laing. A powerful documentary that takes a critical look at the institutionalization of childbirth practices from the viewpoints of the mother and child.

    57 minutes, color
    16-mm: sale, $660; rent $100
    videocasette: sale, $495

Available from:
    Films Incorporated
    733 Green Bay Road
    Wilmette, IL 60091
    800-323-4222
    In Illinois, call collect (312) 256-3200

Birth Without Violence reviews Dr. Frederick Leboyer's gentle birth procedure to minimize birth trauma. 1975.

    21 minutes, black-and-white
    16-mm: sale, $250; rent, $40 plus $6 shipping
    videocassette: not available

Loving Hands is a Leboyer film on touching and massage of newborns to aid the infant in releasing tension, breathing more freely, and bonding. 1976.

    color film
    16-mm: sale, $325; rent, $40 plus $6 shipping

Both available from:
    New Yorker Films
    16 West 61st Street
    New York, NY 10023
    (212) 247-6110

Also of Interest

Tapes from:
 Creative Source
 P.O. Box 11024
 Costa Mesa, CA 92627
 (714) 722-7375

LOVE CHORDS: Music for the Pregnant Mother and Her Unborn Child. A deluxe record album prepared under the direction of Dr. Thomas R. Verny in collaboration with Sandra Collier. For more information contact:

 A & M Records of Canada Limited
 939 Warden Avenue
 Scarborough, Ontario M1L 4C5
 Canada